Like the Sunshine

GW00702033

To dear Mary with love + best wishes Susan

Like the Sunshine

Lieta Betoño
at the dawn of Focolare in Ireland

Susan Gately

newcity
ireland

Published 2013 by

New City Ireland

Focolare Centre, Curryhills House, Prosperous,
Kildare, Ireland

newcityireland@gmail.com

tel: +353-86-8628601

www.focolare.ie

Copyright 2012 © Susan Gately

ISBN 978-0-9575529-0-6

Preface

Essence

How to catch the essence of a person on a page?

Lieta.

A thousand pictures. A thousand facets. Lieta in relax mood in her t-shirt and track pants ready to play tennis; Lieta flipping steaks on a barbeque outside the back door under a sun umbrella, while the blessed Irish summer rain pours down in sheets; Lieta working hard at the computer, ticking off the tasks that are the will of God and must be done; Lieta at prayer; Lieta listening to you with complete stillness, and in front of her emptiness you find the words to express yourself completely and feel completely understood; the wrath of Lieta when you have not done your part and expected others to do it for you; the simplicity of Lieta when she asks you to start again, or sends you a note declaring her readiness to lay down her life for you; the fun of Lieta when she takes up Irish and insists on greeting everyone who comes to the focolare[1] 'as Gaeilge' in peals of laughter; the spontaneity of Lieta, who drops everything when she realises someone is passing through a difficult moment, to visit her or

---

[1] focolare - house where a group of core members of the Focolare Movement live together in community.

call her on the phone; the practicality of Lieta who rolls up her sleeves to clean someone's house; the warmth of Lieta who makes every person she meets feel special, because she loves with her heart; the humour of Lieta, who just weeks before her death can joke about the patch over her eye: "I am the first pirate focolarina[2]" ; the faithfulness of Lieta who fell in love with Jesus and left everything to follow Him when she was just seventeen and remained faithful to that one love all her life.

For thirty years Lieta lived in Ireland. For twenty years she was like a spiritual mother there of the Focolare Movement, generating hundreds and hundreds of people to live the spirituality of unity.

This is her story.

---

[2] Focolarino/a, plural focolarini/e- male/female members of a small core community of the Focolare.

Chapter 1

Childhood

31st January 2008. The President of Ireland, Mary McAleese, ascended the four steps to the large Georgian House, formerly Curryhills House Hotel. It was a cold, dark January evening, but the illuminated house and smiling faces lined up to greet her radiated warmth and love. At the top of the steps, a group of children holding flowers shouted out their joyful greeting. Inside, as she passed from room to room, the President was introduced to small groups of people from the Focolare movement - core members who had left everything to bring its spirituality of unity to the world; families who had moved from Dublin, Cork and Kilkenny to Prosperous in County Kildare, to help build Ireland's first 'little town'; members of the Focolare community from all over Ireland.

A packed meeting room awaited the President's entrance. As she came through the door, people stood, applauding and singing "Every day is a miracle day". They had travelled from the four corners of Ireland to be there. Downstairs another throng of people watched live via video link. For the Focolare movement in Ireland, a little bit of history was in the making: the President of Ireland was celebrating the tenth anniversary of its centre at Prosperous, Co. Kildare.

Four years earlier, on 20th February 2004, Chiara Lubich, founder and President of Focolare had stood in the same room for the official inauguration of the centre. When first purchased in 1998 she had given it the name, "Mariapolis[3] Radiosa", but that day, she renamed it "Mariapolis Lieta." Now President McAleese, on behalf of the people of Ireland, was paying tribute to the movement and to the woman who gave her life to see its spirituality put down roots in Irish soil - Lieta Betoño.

This is a place that radiates, that witnesses love, said President McAleese. "It makes it real and plants it in the lives of those who live here, and then offers it as a gift to the wider community and to our country." But the movement was older than the ten years it had been present at Curryhills House, she said. "The Focolare's journey, Lieta's journey goes much, much further back..."

To tell that story, we must go back to 1951, to La Plata, a city rich in culture near Buenos Aires in Argentina.

Lieta was born Blanca Betoño on 18th June 1951, the sixth child in a family of nine. Her parents had a deep Christian faith, although she admitted herself that she did not recall them talking much of religion. "But they loved us a lot, " she said. Both her grandparents had emigrated from Spain and her parents were distantly related to each other. At a young age her father, Tiburcio and his brothers and

---

[3] Mariapolis - literally 'City of Mary' is the name given to summer and other gatherings of the Focolare Movement.

sisters were sent to a home for needy children. Later he and his brothers were sent to a religious seminary as "interns" and the girls went to convent school on the same basis. As a result Blanca had a host of uncles and aunts who were priests and nuns. Tiburcio did not have a religious vocation and as soon as he met Blanca's mother, Carmen, he left the seminary.

Theirs was a great and pure love which lasted their whole lives. Many years later the children found a letter Tiburcio wrote to Carmen, declaring his love for his wife, with a tenderness and respect that is rare today.

Together they formed a Christian family, Carmen inculcating Christian values, Tiburcio bearing witness to them with his example, although he only went to church on certain occasions.

Though not wealthy, the family was happy. Tiburcio went out to work each day in the civil service and supplemented his income playing the organ for solemn ceremonies in the church. Carmen stayed at home to look after the family. Life in the Betoño home revolved around the kitchen. One by one the children were born and grew: Eduardo, Jorge, Maria Cecilia, Maria del Carmen (called Neldi), Mercedes, Blanca (Lieta), Eugenio (called Mele), Maria Angelica and Maria Isabel, called Kuqui.

Carmen was an astute woman and a fine administrator. With such a large family, they had to work hard to make ends meet, but they did. A childless couple brought them second hand clothes belonging to their nieces and nephews and the family never lacked what they needed to live in a dignified way.

The house had five bedrooms. The boys, Eduardo, Jorge and Eugenio were in two small rooms. The six girls shared another two, and Tiburcio and Carmen were in the fifth bedroom. After a while Tiburcio's Dad, a builder, came to live with them, and built an extension. The large multi-purpose room became a study for the children, a place to entertain their friends and Tiburcio's music room for practising the harmonium.

The Betoño home vibrated with life and thronged with their own children, and their children's friends. Carmen preferred to have the children by her side, where she could keep an eye on them, rather than have them go to other people's houses. At night time, while Tiburcio practised the harmonium, Carmen did the ironing or prepared meals for the next day.

The weather in La Plata was mild and humid, so the family spent a lot of time outdoors. The children played on a swing and trapeze built by their grandfather. In spring and summer, they ate outdoors and Tiburcio tended his vegetable patch or picked fruit from the prune and fig trees. Carmen collected eggs from the henhouse in the corner.

Among the Betoño nine there was always a great affection and a fierce sense of family loyalty. Life had its ups and downs and regularly sparks flew between the children. Eduardo, the eldest son, kept rabbits and after a while they produced a litter of cute baby rabbits. One day when he was out, the younger Betoño children picked up the baby rabbits and cuddled them. When they gave them back to the mother, she rejected and killed them. Eduardo found out and was furious. Blanca and the little ones were in the doghouse for days.

Their strong temperaments led to lots of fights, but they also loved and defended each other to the death. No one picked a fight with a Betoño. An attack on one was an attack on all!

As a child, Blanca was described as "lovable, but stubborn". Once she set her mind on a course of action there was no deterring her, and at times this caused friction at home. But mingled with her stubbornness was a sweetness that ensured she always got her own way in the end, in spite of being one of the youngest. She showed great strength of character even at a young age. When she was five her ankles became swollen with rheumatism and the doctor sent her to hospital, worried that the condition might affect her heart. There she stayed alone in a big hospital ward. Neldi, her older sister, admitted to a little twinge of jealousy, seeing how well she could cope with the pain and the loneliness, though her overriding emotion was one of enormous sympathy as they left her alone in the hospital ward.

Carmen, her mother, was upset to leave her beloved daughter. Together with Neldi they went to the hospital chapel. In silence Carmen knelt and cried her heart out over her little daughter who was so alone. Blanca spent two months in the hospital. During that time she could not walk or put her foot to the ground, but eventually she was well enough to go home. What a celebration greeted her return. A short time later she made her first communion. She was very happy. A huge smile lit up her face, which was chubbier than usual because of the many steroids she had taken during her illness.

Even as a child she had a great love for the most disadvantaged people and would do anything she could to help them. According to her sister Mercedes, it was as if she had taken the unconscious decision already then, to take upon herself the sufferings of other people. She was well liked at school and did not get into trouble, but this was not the case for her older sister, Neldi who was going to have such a profound effect on Blanca's life.

When Blanca was eight, Neldi was twelve and although not yet a teenager, she began to go through a strong crisis of faith. She went to Mass, listened to the readings, was sometimes struck by the Gospel, but she thought it was impossible to live it. She looked at her school friends. Many of them had no faith, and yet they lived better lives than she did. She started to question the existence of God. By age fifteen, she had decided to leave the Church because, as she said, it was of "no benefit" to her. She did not discuss her decision with her parents but the crisis affected her school work and as a result, she missed a whole year of school.

At a party one night Neldi ended up dancing with a young man. There was something different about him. He invited her to meet a group of young people from Catholic Action[4] where she met a young seminarian. There was something different about him too! She asked herself what it all meant. When the seminarian became a priest, he invited Neldi to a gathering of young people and it was there that she had her first contact with the Focolare movement.

A young woman told the story of the movement to a group of around 40 young people. Neldi felt it was like a work of theatre, as if she was watching a play and she was in that play. The woman spoke of the discovery that God is love, that everything else crumbles, the discovery of the presence of Jesus in each person. "I felt these curtains had opened on my life, and perhaps Jesus had come to tell me, 'This is the way to find me - in your brother, you will find me here,'" she recalls.

Neldi's joy was immense, she was transformed.

_____

[4] Catholic Action - the umbrella name given to the variety of iniatives of lay involvement in the Church. In some countries, like Argentina, it took the form of a parish or diocesan structure for lay people co-operating with the clergy in the mission of the Church.

When she went home, she immediately told her Mum and the others of her discovery, and her life took off in a new direction. Blanca, now aged twelve, watched her older sister. Neldi started studying again and in their well-run home, where each child had his or her own chores, she began to do unaccustomed acts of kindness for the others.

At that time, because there were so many of them at home, they took it in turns to cook and wash up at lunch time and in the evening. Each person respected the rigid rota. One evening it was her older sister Cecilia's turn to wash the dishes. She was watching TV and during the ads running in to do the chores. Neldi told her to enjoy the programme, and she would do the dishes. Her sister's eyes widened in surprise. That wasn't part of the deal.

Blanca noticed that Neldi did things in a different way. Before, when Neldi brushed Blanca's hair, she tore at the knots to get it brushed as quickly as possible. Now it was different. She took her time, brushing her hair gently, working out the knots from the bottom, holding her hair above the tangles so that she would not feel any pain.

At a certain point Neldi began to go to Mass every day - something that was unusual at the time. One day, Blanca asked to come along and together they walked the 1,500 metres to the church. Neldi was aged 17, Blanca 13. Along the road that day, Blanca said, "Why don't you tell me your experiences?

What are you living?" Neldi stopped for a moment, because it was like baring her soul. While she had happily chatted away at home, she kept the deeper things of her heart well hidden. "Confiding in Blanca was like breaking a shell, breaking through that human respect that exists between sisters."

But Jesus was present in her sister too, Neldi thought. She was another Jesus to be loved, so she took the step, and began to speak of what she was living. She shared her soul and Blanca remained enchanted, and when they got home afterwards, she said to Neldi, "From now on, I want to live like this, like you. Together with you I want to live in this way."

Now in the Betoño home, Blanca joined her sister in the race to love. They would sit around the table with the whole family having their meal at night. If a row broke out, they would gently kick each other under the table to remind each other to love.

When Neldi was seventeen she felt that Jesus was calling her to give her life to him and a year later she left home to go to complete her studies at a formation school for focolarini in Italy. As she left home, Blanca whispered to her, "I'll take your place now at home."

Later she would write: "From that time, I had to start taking my steps, alone....."

Chapter 2

Lieta's choice

After Neldi's departure for Italy in 1965, life returned to normal in the Betoño household: Carmen, the thrifty mother, making thousands of sacrifices so the children would get a good education; Tiburcio, the hard working father, writing down bookings to play the organ for weddings and funerals in his planner beside the telephone. On great occasions, hidden behind the enormous organ in the huge neo-Gothic cathedral of La Plata, Tiburcio Betoño would perform.

But 1965 was also a year marked by tragedy. On the 3rd of November Blanca's brother Jorge was killed in a tragic air accident over the Bermuda Triangle. The family was devastated by the loss. Blanca began to think very seriously about her own life. It too could end at any moment. She was young, yes, but her brother had been young too and now he was gone, his life was over. Looking at her life stretching before her, she felt urged to make a new choice, her own choice in life - the choice of radical love proposed in the Gospel.

She was struck by the sentence, "Before presenting your gift at the altar, go and be reconciled with your brother." At the time she had a brother who was going through a wild phase. The others were washing their hands of him, but she decided to make a special effort to befriend him. In the evening, she would wait for him, cook dinner and sit with him afterwards. She wanted him to feel her love.

The youth branch of the Focolare, the Gen[5], was coming to life and at age 16 Blanca threw herself into the new initiative. Fiery and enthusiastic, she wanted to be in the thick of the new reality. Along with a few other young people she was invited to move to Buenos Aires to live in a house with some of the other Gen so that together they could spread this Gospel revolution. She asked her parents' permission - could she do her final years of school at Buenos Aires? Looking at their daughter's expectant face, so full of hope and joy - they took the step to let her go. Later she wrote: "Without realising it, I changed school, I changed city and I left home - forever."

Blanca was a person of integrity. There were no half measures. When she decided to live for the Gospel, that meant 100 per cent. Before she left her home, she thought over her life: the people she did not like, the boys who pulled her pigtails at school. She wanted to start with a clean slate in Buenos Aires. That meant having nothing on her conscience as she left. But then, she questioned herself, why should I apologise - they were the ones who hurt me? Yet she knew she had to go the extra mile.

_____

[5] Gen, short for 'New Generation' - the branch of the Movement for young adults.

So one by one, she went to their homes, said good-bye and wished them well. Now she could start a new adventure free of regrets for the past.

Her mother accompanied her on the journey to Buenos Aires, helping to carry her suitcase. Blanca was very happy, her mother a little sad. "Maybe she had already understood that she had to lose me," she later wrote.

She spent the next two years in Avellaneda, a city south of Buenos Aires, completing her education, playing sports and living in the first 'Gen house'. There the girls underwent a period of special formation in the spirituality of the Focolare, called a 'Gen school'. In her spare time she did housework for a woman called Ester, whose daughter had MS. They were finding it very hard to manage but according to Ester, Blanca's arrival was like the arrival of sunshine in their home. It was during that time, when she worked unpaid for them, that they discovered the love of God in the midst of their gnawing suffering.

At the Gen school Blanca shared a bedroom with a sixteen year old girl called Marines. Immediately Blanca became like her older sister. She realised that Marines was coping with lots of changes, for example she had grown up in the country and was now living for the first time in the city. Blanca stood up for her while at the same time encouraging Marines to be independent.

Her great love was sports. She was a natural athlete and dreamt of a future working as a PE instructor. She loved ball games and athletics especially one hundred metres and hurdles. When she played, she played with all her being but though she liked to win, she had a deep feeling for team play too and a great sense of fun - urging her team mates on, passing the ball to everyone, not blaming others if they made a mistake.

Walking through the streets of Buenos Aires, she often saw people without food or shoes and was moved by their plight. She was deeply sensitive to the appalling social problems and did what she could to help with her limited means. The temptation, she confided years later, was to throw herself into social actions for the poor. Instead she realised that she had to do what God wanted of her. She was convinced that if she lived for the accomplishment of Jesus' prayer, 'May they all be one', that this would lead to the resolution of the social problems in her country. For her part that meant being ready to take upon herself the sufferings of the people around her - the people she met each day at the school, on the bus, in the shops. For each one, Blanca vowed, she would be ready to give her life, like Jesus did on the cross.

In a letter from 1970 she wrote: "Today I believe I have to love Jesus forsaken[6] more than ever, looking at humanity, and have as my aim, the vocation 'That all may be one'."

---

[6] Jesus who cries out on the cross "My God, my God, why have you forsaken me?" Matt: 18:46, Mark 15:34

Coming towards the end of her studies, Blanca planned a career as a PE teacher in La Plata. She had done lots of training but had overlooked one important element - the compulsory swimming test. Blanca had never learnt how to swim. Nonetheless, she decided to take the test. How difficult could it be after all? She lined up with all the others, and when told to go, threw herself into the water, promptly sinking to the bottom. She ended up clinging to the boy in the next lane, who rescued her. She failed the test. For now at least there would be no PE college for her.

Her period at the Gen school was coming to a close too and she wondered what her way in life would be. It would be nice to be married and to live very close to a focolare centre - maybe across the road. Then again, she felt a strong attraction for the way of life that had already drawn her sister Neldi to become a core member of a focolare.

These core communities, small groups of men or women who have consecrated their lives to God, shared a life according to the charism of unity, as discovered by Focolare founder, Chiara Lubich. They tried in particular to base their whole lives on having the presence of Jesus spiritually among them (cf Mt. 18:20) in order to be a witness of his presence in the world, supporting themselves through work, and trying to bring the life they were living in the focolare to all the people they met in their day to day lives. The focolare centres were then, and are still today the beating heart of the Focolare movement.

Blanca decided that until she had found her 'way', she would live as if she were a focolarina. She had a chat with Lia, an older member of the focolare community, very experienced in the spiritual life. In tears, she said her yes - she would give her life completely to God. "I cried because I felt the cut I'd be making with my plans, my feelings, with everything. But I cried above all because the love of Jesus is too strong and it asks for everything," she wrote in a letter to Chiara Lubich, the Focolare founder. The letter marked the beginning of a lifelong correspondence.

Shortly after, Blanca followed in her sister Neldi's footsteps, and set off for Loppiano in Italy. This little town, nestling in the Tuscan hills, lies about 30 kilometres south of Florence and was the first little town of the Focolare.

The idea of the 'cittadella' or 'little town' came to the movement's founder in 1961 when on a visit to Switzerland, she saw the town of Einsiedeln which grew up around the Benedictine Abbey and seemed to incarnate St Benedict's ideal of 'Pray and Work'. How would her ideal, 'May they all be one', be embodied? To her mind came the thought of a town - with homes, businesses, schools, factories - all bearing witness to the ideal of unity. The dream became a reality three years later when a close friend received an inheritance of land near

Florence, and Loppiano was born. Today the little town has over 800 inhabitants with a college, houses, a town hall, workshops, a church, a business park and the newly established Sophia University Institute. But when Blanca went to Loppiano in October 1970, it was much smaller and its main focus was as the location for the two year formation course preparing men and women to enter focolare communities. Yet the atmosphere was the same - the atmosphere generated when people loved each other.

Blanca threw herself into life in Loppiano. Forty five young women were there at the Focolare school of formation. She was one of the youngest. Immediately she settled down to live in one of the small focolare communities and started work at the Centro Ave Art centre. Her days were well ordered routines of work, study, sport, prayer but above all, building up relationships, one by one, with those around her. Blanca described it as a "paradise of extraordinary life".

She continued her correspondence with the movement's founder describing her life and the steps she was taking in her spiritual journey. In one letter she described how she only wanted to "give joy to others" and she asked Chiara for a special sentence from the Gospel to guide her life. Chiara's reply two months later would stamp on Blanca the characteristic that would always be hers: joy. The sentence that the founder of Focolare chose for her was:

"Brothers, we wish you happiness; try to grow perfect; help one another." (2 Cor. 13:11) and from that sentence came the name with which Blanca became known: Lieta (the Italian word for happy or joyful). In reality joy was always a characteristic of Blanca, but now with this new name, it seemed to become her essence and something she was able to share with all around her. In a letter afterwards she wrote: "With all my heart I want to bear witness to God who is song, joy, life by always choosing ever more, Jesus forsaken, on all the occasions when He is present."

As time passed in Loppiano, Lieta matured as a person. She gained a new understanding of love. Whereas at the beginning she felt the presence of God very strongly impelling her to love all the people around her with enthusiasm, after a time, she did not experience His presence, which had given her such joy, in the same way, and felt she was losing Him. She saw how incapable she was and experienced all her frailties. She realised love was not just a matter of feelings. You do not love God and others just to be good, to feel at ease or even to make other people happy. You love God for Himself. You enter that 'why?' of Jesus on the cross and stay there with Him. You choose Him, not the joy of the friendship and unity with the others and it is "beautiful to look for Him and be vigilant" when He arrives.

The way she related to the people around her changed. One day she was with a friend who had a problem and was suffering. Initially Lieta searched around for words to console her, but then realised she had none. This was a moment for silence, for immersing herself in her friend's pain. They sat down. Lieta understood she had to love God himself in her friend's suffering. As her friend spoke, Lieta emptied her mind of everything, and listened to her right to the end. She gave no answers, but in the end, her capacity to understand other people and enter their sufferings had grown, and they were both at peace.

In the winter of 1972, Lieta and her friends left Loppiano. One by one they heard where they were going in the world. Lieta was destined for Ireland.

Writing just before she left Rome for her new homeland, she admitted to a slight sense of fear, but was also full of excitement and expectation. "I lack nothing. I have a father, a mother and my spouse and a great family to love."

Chapter 3

Ireland

What went through Lieta's mind when in the dead of winter, she arrived by boat in Dublin in 1972? She had lived in the warm and dusty land of Argentina, and in the beautiful Tuscan hills of Northern Italy. Ireland was different. Dark and overcast, green, cold and rainy. But the people were warm and welcoming and immediately she felt at home.

Now aged 21, she had long black hair, a hypnotic smile and lively, warm brown eyes that crinkled at the corners when she smiled. Such was her warmth that it came as spontaneous for people to embrace her whenever they met her, although this was quite alien to the culture at the time. Generally when people greeted each other they shook hands.

Originally Lieta lived in a small basement flat in a Georgian house in south Dublin with Aurea from Italy and Mary from Liverpool. It was the movement's first centre, really more like a 'pied à terre', or foothold. It had a small sitting room, a kitchenette and two small bedrooms. It was unfurnished, so they sat on bright orange cushions on the floor in the sitting room. A few interesting pictures strategically placed on the wall made it feel bright and modern. It was very sparse and quite damp.

The wider community consisted of a middle aged woman, Margaret Neylon who had met the movement in Liverpool and moved to Dublin, her son Eddie who was in a wheelchair, a number of his friends, and a couple of priests, including Fr. Ed Grimes, a Spiritan Father, who was chaplain to two girls' schools in Dublin.

Each day Aurea went out to a job in a jam factory where she worked removing the stems from oranges. Mary worked as an interpreter with the Irish livestock board. Lieta had no English so her first task was to learn it - a task she undertook with great good humour and much laughter. Often she would cycle to Margaret Neylon's house, which was close by, for conversation classes.

One of her first weekends there, a group of around ten girls came to visit the focolare from Mount Sackville school where Fr Grimes was chaplain. They were aged between 15 and 17 and a little intrigued by the rather simple flat they were visiting, and its unusual inhabitants. At the time in Ireland there were very few foreigners, so to meet a community of three women from Argentina, Italy and Britain was most unusual.

Aurea and Mary held the meeting for the girls who sat cross-legged on the cushions. At the end they made a reel to reel tape for the 'gen' in England, telling them what they were doing and how they too wanted to live the revolution of the Gospel.

In the small kitchenette at the back of the flat, Lieta was making coffee and learning her first words of English: "Would you like a cup of coffee," which she repeated time and time again with a smile, working in particular on her pronunciation of "would". The girls, and I was one of them, were immediately entranced by her warmth, her love and her humour.

After a few months Lieta and the others moved a few doors up the road to a bigger and slightly less damp apartment at 48 Terenure Road East. Aurea left for a focolare centre in Portugal and Pina Peduzzi from Milan arrived to take her place.

At the time, Ireland was economically poor and a bastion of traditional Catholicism. Catholic churches were packed to the porch doors every Sunday, and there was a huge weekday Mass-going population too. More than half the population was under 25, but as soon as young people completed their studies, even for the summer, they went abroad looking for work.

In the north of Ireland, the 'troubles' which had exploded into violence on the streets in 1969 were escalating. The first radio news bulletin each day, announced a bombing, a riot, a murder, a tit for tat punishment beating. Through the day, further details of that day's atrocity would be uncovered, ready for full exposition on the evening television news. The next day would bring new horror. While the troubles were only a few hours up the road from Dublin, the atmosphere in the city was much calmer and people tried to get on with their lives and forget about the north, until a particularly gruesome atrocity would shock them out of their complacency.

The Focolare movement's ideal of unity was a very new concept for such a traditional Catholic country, whose missionaries had helped to spread the Gospel throughout the world. Pina immediately realized that in order to impact the Irish people, they had to show the Gospel being lived collectively, together. People had to be able to say of the three of them: "See how they love one another."

One day Pina, Lieta and Mary made a pact to be always ready to die for each other so that Jesus would be present among them, as he said in Matthew's Gospel "Where two or more are gathered in my name, I am there in their midst." (Mt 18:20) The Irish had already seen people who loved, now they had to see people who loved each other.

The three women became the heart of a vibrant focolare community in Dublin. There was no men's focolare centre, so the whole community gathered regularly in the small basement apartment. The atmosphere in Ireland's first focolare was very special.

"Going to the focolare was like going to Paradise," recalls Fr Brendan Purcell one of the priests who got to know the movement at that time. "You met

Jesus in the midst going through the door, not Pina, Mary and Lieta."

The apartment was in a redbrick house set back from the road and accessed through a door under the steps which lead up to the main house. Directly outside the gate was a bus stop. Their first task when they moved in was to give the flat the stamp of beauty. Lieta joined the others in painting the walls a warm butter colour. They hung a guitar on the wall, and Pina, who was doing a course on carpentry each Monday night, set about building shelves. But transporting the long planks of wood for the shelves proved to be a challenge. In the end, they opted for the bus, and as a bewildered bus driver and conductor looked on, they placed the upright planks through the gap in the spiral staircase! With disarming smiles, they asked the conductor was this ok? He had not the heart to refuse, and the planks made it back to the focolare centre intact.

The landlady was much impressed by the simple but tasteful changes the three women made to the apartment. Even the back bedroom where Lieta slept, which was a cacophony of colours - flowery carpet, stripy bedspread - was somehow transformed, when after a number of trips by bus back and forth to a carpet shop, the three women agreed on a plain, rich one-tone brown carpet. So much so that a visitor who saw the room a little later said, "But this is like a first class hotel!"

Gerry Steele, one of the first Gen from Belfast, recalls meeting Pina, Lieta and Mary in the basement apartment. "There was a definite order, harmony, sense of something unusual, something novel. I thought they were very beautiful girls, very attractive as was the way they spoke to each other. There was harmony, friendship and joy."

As people got to hear about the movement, either by word of mouth, or through for example, a short radio report, there were regular curious visitors to the focolare centre.

One of these was Marian Gillegan, one of the first Irish Gen. She met the Focolare through Eddie McCaffrey with whom she shared a special bond, as she too had muscular dystrophy. Early in 1973 she visited the focolare centre, where she met Pina, Mary and Lieta. Lieta had only been in Ireland a month or two. Pina told the story of the movement while Lieta listened intently. Marian, aged 19 at the time, knew Lieta did not speak or understand English and wondered how someone who did not understand anything could look so interested and be so enthusiastic!

Lieta had a great capacity to give people a belief in themselves. When she met Marian's brother Pádraic, a young teenager starting to play guitar, she encouraged him to write a song for a song contest at the summer gathering (Mariapolis) of the Focolare in England that year. "Her English was pretty awful but she communicated such boundless joy and enthusiasm with her eyes that I started to believe I could actually write a song," he recalls. Afterwards Pádraic and a number of friends went on to write many songs, and to form a band, Factor 1, which produced four albums.

While Pina and Mary went out to work each day, Lieta was now attending English language classes in a college. It was her first year living as part of a focolare community, and seen as a try out period to see if she was cut out for the life. She soon hit her first test. At the college where she was learning English, she attracted a serious admirer. She too felt an attraction for the man. What should she do? She realised the attraction was becoming a temptation pulling her away from the life choice she had undertaken. She did not hesitate, but immediately went to Pina, who was the person responsible for the Dublin focolare centre, and told her about it. She shared so that she could see in the light of unity what to do. Once she shared the attraction, it was gone and became, instead of an obstacle, a source of a more open and honest unity between her and Pina. What was more, her mind was no longer impacted by thoughts of the man. Instead she experienced a new interior freedom that allowed her to love each person she met.

Mary was now working at the Irish offices of Fiat and through her work Lieta got a part time job cleaning the house of Fiat's director in Ballsbridge, a rich area of Dublin. She also looked after children. She tried to bring the atmosphere of love they were living in the focolare to all the people she met outside. "I have to be like a mother to other people", she wrote.

She was ready to let go of anything that did not increase the presence of Jesus in the focolare. She'd have loved to do judo for example, but for a whole lot of reasons, it wasn't the right time for that, so she gave up that idea. But as time went by, she saw that everything she let go of for God, came back to her. She let judo go, and discovered instead a great ability and passion for racket sports like tennis and badminton which she played regularly. She let go of her family in Argentina and found a new family in Ireland. She let go of a possible boyfriend and experienced the freedom of the children of God and a greater Love.

Pina did all she could to make sure Lieta's first year living in the focolare centre was a happy one and that she was really made for this way of life. She felt there was no doubt at all about Lieta's call and desire to respond to it, but realized that Lieta needed to complete her education so as to be humanly mature. So Pina helped her further her education, suggesting she study Irish history and politics. Lieta was like a sponge, soaking everything in and wanting to learn.

In December 1973 the first year was up. Lieta said she had no doubts. Living in the focolare was what she wanted to do for her life. It was simple, she said, because "I have given my life to Jesus forever".

Meanwhile, the troubles in the North of Ireland got worse by the day. In Argentina, Lieta had taken the step to believe that the ideal of unity would solve the social problems. In Ireland the challenge was to believe that this spirituality could contribute to peace in the north.

One day, with the faith of children, Pina, Mary and Lieta asked in the name of Jesus that a way would open up for the spirituality of unity to enter Northern Ireland. A few days later an Anglican nun, Sr Anna, rang from Belfast. She was planning to bring a group of young Catholics and Protestants from the city to a youth festival at the Focolare's little town of Loppiano. She wanted them to have a strong experience of the Gospel which would be an answer for their lives.

Immediately Lieta and the others saw this as God's answer to their prayer. Among the group that travelled was Sally McAllister. She had grown up in a working class area of North Belfast and was on the point of joining the IRA when she went on the trip to Loppiano. The tour completely transformed her vision of life, and even when she was attacked by thugs on her return to Belfast, she did not retaliate, but stuck to the choice of the Gospel she had made in Loppiano.

Sally was living in Belfast, but became a very regular visitor to the focolare in Dublin, regularly sleeping over at weekends. Lieta used to give up her bed, and sleep on the floor. She and Sally were close in age, and both boisterous young people. They liked nothing better than a pillow fight at night time, where they would "absolutely murder each other", recalls Sally.

Often members of the travelling community[7] called to the focolare looking for help. Because she was at home most, Lieta was the one to meet them. She always tried to give them something, either clothes or food and to make them feel welcome. A regular visitor was Sam, a young lad of 15. In 1974 Sally moved to Dublin to be closer to the focolare community. One day she and Lieta were out shopping for essentials for her new flat. She wanted to buy a vegetable knife, but had run out of money. Lieta invited her to trust in providence. "I thought it was a bit daft," Sally recalls, but agreed to wait. A few days later Sam arrived at the focolare and this time, instead of asking for something, he brought a gift - a small vegetable knife.

Lieta's trust in God's love was verified.

---

[7] Members of the travelling community. A traditional nomadic people of ethnic Irish origin. They are known as 'Travellers'

Chapter 4

Training Gospel revolutionaries

Lieta had the heart of a South American revolution-
ary. As a teenager she had thrown her life into the
newborn Gen movement in Argentina. In the 70s as
a young woman, she was to inculcate a generation
of Irish young people with the fire of the Gospel;
the solution to all social problems, the source of real
happiness.

Young people in several universities in Dublin and
in a Catholic college in Belfast who came in touch
with the movement, told their friends about it, and
gradually the circle of people trying to live what
they saw as 'the Gospel revolution' in Ireland grew
larger. In 1975, Lieta accompanied a group to a festival for young people in Rome. She was free and
happy, chatting alternatively with one girl, an air
hostess on her first trip with Focolare, about make-
up and fashion, and with another, about her own
choice not to marry and showing her fulfilment as a
single person.

By now she had mastered English and was working
in a small stationery shop in Stillorgan. She was an
efficient worker, and took her work very seriously,
always ticking things off lists and making sure she

had not forgotten anything. Yet, while she was a hard and conscientious worker, she was always ready to interrupt what she was doing if someone needed her help.

Her role in the movement was to look after the Gen, the young people. "She exuded this amazing sense of the importance of the revolution of the Gen, this new generation that would bring about a united world," recalls Alve Bevan, one of those first Gen. Little by little a circle of young people aged from 16 to 23 began to get together regularly in the focolare, meeting first with Pina, and then after a while, with Lieta. She shared her own stories of life as a Gen back in Argentina, and instilled a sense of enthusiasm and purpose.

She asked a lot from the young people, but loved a lot too. Genny English from Tipperary recalls a weekend where she misled Lieta to avoid coming to a gathering of the Gen. The next time they met, Lieta drew her aside and gently but firmly told her that she didn't think that Genny was telling the truth the last time they spoke. Genny was impressed by her courage to confront her in such a forthright way. "Lieta loved you in the truth," she said.

She also suggested to Genny that Jesus might be calling her to himself. "And he may only call you once," she added. He had called, and Genny followed Lieta in her radical choice of God in the focolare.

There was still no men's focolare centre, so the whole community used to meet in the women's focolare, first in Terenure and then in a house in Ballyroan Crescent, south county Dublin. The Gen boys, some of whom had originally "fancied her like mad" saw Lieta as an ally and "grew to love her as a sister". For the girls, she was like another mother, accompanying them through their trials in life, and guiding them in the Gospel.

Then in 1976, the men's focolare opened and for the first time the Gen boys had the opportunity to meet among themselves with Bruno and two recently arrived focolarini - Terry from New Zealand and Mario from Italy.

On a sunny Saturday afternoon in the summer of that year the Gen girls were meeting with Lieta in the women's focolare in Dublin. By then Mary had left Ireland, and three other women had come to live in the focolare with Lieta and Pina: Arminda from Mozambique, Myriam from the Lebanon and Marie Antonietta from Italy. One of the Gen girls sat upstairs on Lieta's bed for a chat. She was in college, and going through a wild patch. She had started going out with a lecturer who was fourteen years older than her and the relationship with him was drawing her away from Christian values and her life with the Gen, with whom she had shared so much. Lieta was worried about her sensing she was putting herself in what could be a vulnerable situation. As they chatted, she invited her to come to an international meeting for young people that summer. With her head down, the girl refused. She only had a little money, she said. Lieta said they could find the rest of the money, but then she was silent. Her heart went out to the girl whom she loved like a sister, and she began to cry. When the girl saw Lieta's tears trickling down her face she was overcome.

"I was stunned by her tears," she said. "No one had ever loved me to the point of shedding tears for me." Immediately she changed her mind and made a resolution to start again to live the Gospel. She went downstairs and told the others about her change of heart. Shortly after, she stopped seeing the lecturer, and with a great joy, took up her life as a Christian once again.

Lieta did not love at a distance, but got involved in people's lives. In Alve's case, this was particularly when her Mum died through suicide in November 1977. Alve was 17.

Through Alve's grief, Lieta was there, and when she could not be present, she sent some of the others to take care of her and help practically. She insisted Alve go back to school and regularly sent her home from the focolare to do her homework. In the months following her mother's death, Lieta continued to support her. At Easter time, she sat with Alve and they had a chat. At the end she produced an Easter egg. "She knew well that things were not too good at home and she loved me as I needed to be loved, as a kid missing her Mam - Lieta stepped up to the mark."

Even when Alve drifted from the movement, Lieta stayed in touch, challenging her behaviour because she had the courage to love her as she was. "She was always there respecting the space I needed, yet present."

Lieta and the women living in the Dublin focolare had a particular love for the Gen living in Northern Ireland. They had suffered enormously because of the troubles, each of them experiencing profound personal loss and horror. For example, Margaret Agnew, one of the first Gen, went to a lecture in college one day, and the building across the road was blown up, smashing in all the windows of the lecture hall. All that was left of the building opposite was the gable end of the house, where a dazed man now sat on a bed in his pyjamas. There was a thin line between life and death.

Day in, day out the Gen from Belfast lived with violence and mistrust. They saw the spirituality of the Focolare as the antidote to the animosity so present in society. In Belfast you had to be very careful about who you got to know. But here was a Gospel spirituality which taught the opposite. A shaft of light in a dull sky.

Lieta and the others tried to make the Gen from Belfast feel their love in every way possible.

"When the Gen come from Belfast we try to keep them in the focolare, at least one or two, so the harmony and the peace of the focolare and the joy of Jesus in the midst might soothe the wounds of suffering that they too feel, living in Northern Ireland," she wrote to a friend. They were in touch all the time by phone and letter. They wanted the Gen in the north to know they were never alone. Pina wrote long letters enflaming them with love, and telling them not to be afraid. Lieta was in touch with them by phone on a regular basis.

She saw the suffering in Northern Ireland as an aspect of Jesus' suffering. In Northern Ireland, so close to where Lieta was living, Jesus was crying out once more "Why have you forsaken me?" But in a letter to a friend, she confided that there was such a presence of God when they met the Gen and the other people of the movement in the North and embraced the difficulties with them, that it became an experience of Paradise.

It was not just a matter of bringing a Gospel based spirituality to them. She and Pina emphasised the human. Did someone need something? Had they warm clothes or enough food. They made things happen. There was no difference between the human and the divine. They would notice things - "You've no decent shoes, you need a new pair".

This was particularly so when a few Gen moved into a small flat in South Parade in Belfast. It was cold and there were no curtains or lampshades, so Pina went off and bought the material and made up the curtains, and they bought lampshades. "Every time they came, they used to bring hampers of food - tins of beans, jars of jam, which they sometimes would have received from the nuns," recalls Margaret Agnew.

They were typical students in the Gen house with very little money, so encouraged by Lieta, the Gen from the south shared with them. "I remember one time Lieta came up with money that one of the Gen had been saving for a new helmet to go with her moped and she gave it to us instead. I was really moved," says Margaret.

In particular they tried to give the Gen in the north a bigger focus - the accomplishment of Jesus' prayer 'May they all be one'. Those who got involved felt they were part of something bigger than the Troubles - they were part of the Christian revolution in the world. Their corner was Northern Ireland, where there was war, but united to the focolare centre in Dublin, they became part of a network that stretched right across the world, where everyone was living for the same ideal of unity, peace and love.

Their personal love, and fiery enthusiasm, gave the Gen in Belfast an extraordinary impetus to spread the spirituality and in the late 70s they were distributing hundreds of copies of the 'Word of Life' (a monthly commentary on a sentence of Scripture), holding meetings, broadcasting a hospital radio show, and running a small youth club for girls (Gen 3) on the Falls Road, the principal road in the Catholic part of Belfast. Lieta had a particular love for these younger girls. Whenever she heard a special piece of news, she would ring Margaret to tell her, and ask her to spread the word around the younger children.

Two of the first Gen from Belfast, Sally McAllister and Juanita Majury, followed Lieta's way and became core members of the focolare.

One day Lieta was at home in Dublin when the phone rang. It was Margaret ringing from Belfast. She was meant to go to Liverpool, but a huge bomb had gone off in the city centre and all the gates were locked. "Don't worry. If we keep Jesus among us you'll be ok," Lieta assured her, making her promise that she would ring when she got home. "She was like a mother," Margaret recalls. "It was a disaster, but I was at peace because I was in the will of God."

By 1980, Lieta had been living eight years in Ireland. In a letter she described her period in Ireland as one of "light and love" where she had grown humanly and in the spiritual life. She goes on, "Do you know that as time passes I fall more and more in love with Jesus. I feel He is becoming flesh of my flesh and soul of my soul. I feel I cannot live without Him."

It was undoubtedly this deep and faithful love for Jesus and her strong unity with the others in the focolare that allowed the movement to grow steadily during those years.

It was not easy. There were constant calls to speak about the movement and constant activities - from smaller group meetings that allowed everyone to share their life, to large youth meetings and summer gatherings.

In the early months of 1981, the whole movement was getting ready for a large youth meeting in Dublin. In every spare moment, Lieta was hard at work with the Gen, inviting young people to the gathering, attending rehearsals, giving lifts and providing accommodation. At one rehearsal she reminded the Gen that what was most important was not the mime they were performing: if they listened to one another's ideas with love, then the mime would be a true expression of unity and this was what counted.

People got tired, emotions got frayed, but somehow Lieta managed to ride the storm, keeping people amused with her funny imitations when the going got tough. "She was a very spiritual person, but she was very funny," Nora, one of those living with her in the focolare centre recalls. "She put a bounce in everything we did."

At night, Lieta, Pina, Mary Frances (a new focolarina from the Philippines) and Nora would sit around the kitchen table, exchanging jokes and laughter over a last cuppa.

Lieta poured enthusiasm and love into the young people she was in touch with, from the southern coastal town of Dungarvan to the north-western island of Aranmore, and they in their turn poured it out on the people around them, inviting their friends to the youth meeting in Dublin.

The Gen in the North had a particular sense of 'apostolic mission' and took advantage of each opportunity to bring busloads of people from Belfast to Dublin. "We looked at the situation here in Northern Ireland and unity was what was needed," said Gerry Steele, one of the first Gen who lived on the troubled Falls Road.

In the end the youth meeting in the RDS attracted more than 1,000 people with busloads arriving from Wicklow, Letterkenny, Belfast, Dungarvan, Kilkenny and Athlone. A major political party was having its AGM in a nearby hall, and IRA supporters noisily protested outside against the hunger strikes in Belfast. Lieta, the Gen and their friends quietly slipped by them, to their own rally, proposing an alternative revolution: the Gospel revolution of love.

1962: Betoño family in a line: from the left: Eduardo (eldest of 9), Jorje, Neldi, Cecilia, Mercedes, Lieta, Mele, Maria Angelica, Kuqui.

Betoños: Left to right (back row): Jorje, Mercedes, Cecilia, Neldi, Eduardo.

Left to right (front row): Mele, Carmen, Kuqui (on her lap), Tiburcio, Maria Angelixca, Lieta.

Lieta aged 12

Picture of Lieta on front of Gen magazine 1968

Mary Frances, Dori Zambone, Ita, Therese, Lieta (in front) and Juanita, November 1986

Talking to Archbishop McNamara: Bruno Carrera, Fran Meagher, Andrew Basquille, Lieta, October 1985

Lieta with Catherine Burke

Lieta gives talk at Mariapolis
in Limerick, summer 1991

Lieta 1992

Lieta surrounded by a group of
focolare members, 1990

Lieta and Neldi

Lieta talks to a
group of Gen 4,
1998

Lieta with Pina and
Mary (the focolarine
with whom she lived
in the first focolare
in Dublin) 1994

Lieta signs deed on
Curryhills House,
with Bruno Carrera,
Liam Travers and
Dan Gallery
16.1.1998

Curryhills house
Mariapolis Lieta

Chapter 5

A Pentecost Experience

In June 1981, Lieta travelled to London. Chiara Lubich had won a prestigious award from the Anglican Church and during her stay in London she was to meet the community of the Focolare from the UK and Ireland.

Before Chiara met everyone, she called together her closest collaborators, the men and women who lived in the focolare centres. There was Mass and then Chiara shared a new understanding she had gained of holiness. Lieta sat in rapt attention on the floor, listening to every word. Chiara said that they had all to become saints together by doing what God wanted in each moment. They had to be like kangaroos, jumping fully from one present moment to the next. She said if they did not become saints, then she would not become a saint either. The catch phrase was 'saints together'. It was a new form of holiness. For Lieta it was a Pentecost experience. She realised her life had to jump to a new level. With her friends she had to aim at being a saint.

The days in London were a powerful injection of life. A busload arrived from Ireland. They had made the long journey by coach and boat. Others flew in from Dublin and Belfast. Almost all the Gen from Belfast were present. For many it was the first time that they personally met with Chiara.

One by one, Chiara answered questions from the Irish, English, Scottish and Welsh communities, ending with a question from the Gen in Belfast. "How did you live during the war?" Her answer surprised everyone. We were so taken with God, with his love, that we didn't even notice the war, she said. "We almost didn't know who was coming into the city, whether it was the Americans or the Germans - who they were. This wasn't of interest to us. We were taken by God. And this Christian revolution was beginning. You too try and do this. And then you will do good to Ireland because Ireland needs Jesus."

"Ireland needs Jesus", echoed in Lieta's heart. "Ireland needs Jesus."

Returning to her job in the Irish Medical Association, although nothing had changed, Lieta was different. She felt the world was made of cardboard and all the things in it were like toys. Only the people of faith, people happy with the things of heaven, "seem like adults. Others they are happy but they don't know what happiness is yet", she wrote in a letter.

At the office she continued to work as normal, sharing what she could about her trip to London. But her colleagues noticed that she was changed. When they were alone, a secretary asked her about the Focolare. With each person she experienced "almost a supernatural relationship as though something was enveloping me. Jesus was happy in them. Everyone drew out things about God, and I hadn't opened my mouth!" she confided later.

Life returned to normal. In the focolare they prepared for the summer gathering (Mariapolis) in Kilkenny. That year for the first time a bus load arrived from Strabane in Northern Ireland, a hot spot of IRA activity with 70 per cent unemployment...a new Focolare community was coming to life. Afterwards Lieta, Pina, Mary Frances and Juanita took their well deserved holidays. Things were quieter in the summer months, and Lieta had more time to play tennis and practise cooking her famous Argentinean 'assados' on the barbeque grill in the back garden, though often it was under the shelter of a big rain umbrella.

When she had time, in the evenings, or sometimes if she was not busy at work and had spare time, she liked to write to her Gen friends around Ireland. Lieta never abandoned anyone who had been touched by the spirituality and tried to immediately share, by phone or letter, what she was living and the news of the movement, so that people would remain faithful to their choice of the Gospel and feel part of a family.

A few months after her "Pentecost experience" in

London, she wrote to seven Gen girls in Dungarvan, a small town on the south coast of Ireland: "Let's not go down, Gen. Let our flame of love for Jesus grow every day and this happens if we love one another. We can't do anything bigger than having Jesus among us. He will then solve the problems of the world but first we have to allow Him to live among us in our love, which is not mere sentimentalism, not at all, it is real."

She urged them to forgive each other in order to start again "The Gen life is not easy but it is fascinating. There are many Gen in the world. You are not alone, so don't get discouraged," she wrote, reminding them that there only needed to be two of them to have the presence of Jesus in their midst.

For young people living in a small rural town like Dungarvan, the Gen revolution opened up the world. "At the time our faith went from being Sunday Mass, to something real, alive and to be lived every day," said Anne Marie Foley, who was aged 19 at that time. "We were from a religious family. The attitude was that you were trying, trying, but with a sense of guilt that you were not getting there, whereas with the Gen, it was to simply love in every present moment."

The relationships Lieta formed with all those Gen 'under her wing' in the 70s and 80s lasted right until the day she died. She did not forget the people entrusted to her, intervening at key moments in their lives - moments of crises and of joy.

Years later a small group of those Gen, Lieta's spiritual daughters, were chatting about the deep impact she had on their lives.

By then they were all married with children. One by one each shared how Lieta had intervened personally to save or strengthen their marriages - encouraging them through moments of difficulty, helping them to start again with their husbands, making them believe in the grace of the sacrament and the power of love to heal relationships. Lieta had loved each one, to the end.

Chapter 6

Change

1982 was a year of change. Lieta had been living in community with Pina for nine years, growing to maturity under the guidance of her great Italian friend with whom she shared an incredible and visible unity.

After the summer gathering in Kilkenny, they were resting and turned their minds to the thought of purchasing a house. The focolare house in Ballyroan Crescent was too small for the movement's burgeoning needs and it was rented, so they could not extend. The time had come to purchase a property.

One day that summer, Pina bought The Irish Times and began to scan the property section. Immediately she spotted a property which ticked all the boxes. It was a fine detached house fifteen minutes from the centre of Dublin, with a large sitting room opening onto a dining room, two other reception rooms and four bedrooms.

The detached house was on a cul de sac with lots of on street parking. Lieta and the others were immediately excited and went with Pina to see the property. Looking at the women emerging from their battered white mini, the auctioneer politely asked: "Do you know how much this property costs?" Pina was not fazed. "We have a rich husband," she whispered to the others.

They loved the house and asked Jesus to give them a sign if He meant them to buy it. They did not have long to wait. The very next day a woman rang the focolare centre. She had received a sum of money in providence and was "thinking it would be useful for a house". "You are really the answer of God," Pina told her. But they were not in a position to put in an offer on the house for some time. Would it wait for them? In great peace, the women entrusted the house to God and set off on their holidays. Lieta was away for the first two weeks in August, totally oblivious to the fact that her life was about to change.

In London, Mari Ponticaccia, who at that time co-directed the movement in Britain and Ireland, needed a secretary and thought of the efficient and talented Lieta. She wanted her to come to London in September. For the first time Lieta faced the hard step of leaving all the people she had grown so attached to, and quitting her job. It was a huge wrench but straight away she said Yes and began her preparations to leave.

At a hastily convened farewell party in the Gen house in Rathfarnham, just down the road from the focolare centre in Ballyroan, the whole community gathered to say goodbye to Lieta. She was suffering but serene. She had said Yes to God, giving Him the gift of her whole life. That meant she had to be ready to go wherever He wanted her. Now He wanted her in London. She did not question but obeyed. Still it was hard to say goodbye.

The community was shocked she was leaving so quickly, but managed to get together a whole selection of presents of things she would like - sporty tops, Irish music, Irish poetry... The young people put together a little concert and recalled key moments in her almost ten years in Ireland. "Stay where you are, don't roam too far. Don't let your footsteps slip into the desert. Keep your feet on the ground, or else we'll go down!" they sang-parodying a song they often sang at meetings. While there was much laughter at their mock gravity, there was also pain. No-one wanted Lieta to leave. Everyone recognised what a precious gift she was and that the relationship built with her over the years, would remain.

Days before she left, Margaret, a young teacher from Dublin, came to live in the focolare centre in Ballyroan Crescent. It was a Monday, and Lieta was to leave the following Friday.

As Pina worked in another room, Lieta quietly called Margaret and Mary Francis aside. Like an older sister telling her younger siblings how to act with their mother, she passed on to them the benefit of her experience. She urged them to always be united with Pina, to let go of personal judgements and concentrate on keeping the presence of Jesus in the midst in the focolare. Margaret never forgot her words, and just as having the presence of God in the focolare had been Lieta's priority, from that moment it became hers too. Meanwhile, Lieta was throwing herself into the new adventure of life in London.

On Friday 1st October 1982, she arrived, suitcase in hand, at the focolare centre in Thurleigh Road. This was the women's zone centre for England, Scotland, Wales and Ireland[8]. Two other women were living there with Mari. She already knew them well and they welcomed her with open arms. Immediately she was at home. Mari was leaving for Rome within a few weeks, so while practical arrangements were being made concerning Lieta, she lived out of a suitcase, helping wherever she could and awaiting Mari's return from Rome to work out a definite practical timetable for her life.

She set off for Manchester to help with a retreat for a hundred Cross and Passion sisters. At first the nuns were taken aback because she was so young, but as soon as she started sharing her own stories of living the Gospel, they were moved by her spiritual maturity and enthusiasm. Next she moved into the focolare centre in Liverpool, where she helped her friends there to look for a new house.

---

[8] The Focolare worldwide is divided into geographical regions called 'zones'. At the time Ireland was part of the zone of 'Great Britain and Ireland' with its centre in London.

Meanwhile in Rome, a new initiative was being set in motion that would have huge implications for Lieta's future. Each October Chiara Lubich met with the delegates of the movement from all over the world in a recap and planning month-long conference. The movement was young in Ireland so it was run from London, where it had been present for a much longer period. As usual that year the two delegates for Britain and Ireland, Mari and Dimitri, set off armed with reports, pictures and statistics on how the movement was progressing in the various places. But nothing was to stay the same after this particular meeting, which came to be known in Focolare circles as 'The October Revolution'.

The 'revolution' was a new structuring of the movement around zone centres where the most mature and experienced focolare members would live. This meant in effect that the current directors of the focolare centres in England, Scotland, Wales and Ireland, would move to the zone centre in London to live with Mari, and the responsibility for the focolare centres would pass to younger members, like Lieta.

Pina Peduzzi, who had led the focolare in Ireland for ten years, and who was in the throes of finalising the sale of the new focolare centre at Ramleh Close, in the Dublin suburb of Milltown, was now to live in London; Lieta was to return to Ireland, just weeks after her departure, to take Pina's place.

Pina had been an incredible leader of the movement in Ireland. Naturally fiery, intelligent and full of love, she had a charismatic attraction and light. People could not imagine the focolare without her, but as she herself explained it to the Irish community, it became clear that it was truly what God wanted in that moment.

But while Pina put a brave face on it, she was heartbroken to be leaving Ireland and struggled painfully with the decision. Lieta now found herself back in Ireland. While delighted to be back, she was faced with a whole new situation. She could understand the pain Pina felt at leaving a country where she had been a pioneer of the movement. She knew Pina was happy that she was taking her place, but both women still experienced a huge wrench. "Jesus has asked everyone for huge 'cuts', and love for Jesus forsaken is the only compass who helps us to go forward always," wrote Pina in her final updating report to the centre of the movement in Rome. A little while later, she was welcomed to London, as Lieta had been, and began adjusting to life there.

Back in Dublin, Lieta suddenly found herself responsible for the little focolare centre of Mary Frances, Margaret and Juanita, and together with Bruno, for the larger movement. For a young woman of 31, she had a lot on her shoulders. She was in regular contact with Pina (who still acted as advisor for Ireland), and conscious that she was suffering the pain of separation. Lieta tried to live each day, one moment at a time, entrusting her friend to God.

Then one night the phone rang, and to Lieta's surprise, it was Pina's mother ringing from Milan. She assured Lieta that all that was happening - Pina's departure and her own new responsibility, was part of God's loving plan.

"Be at peace," she told Lieta, "You are doing the will of God." This voice out of the blue gave her great consolation.

Chapter 7

Learning to be a spiritual mother

Weeks after Lieta left Ireland for London, she was back. With a smile she greeted everyone at the door of the new focolare centre in Milltown. People pulled her leg at the short absence. Fr Brendan Purcell told her she would have to give her presents back!

"I am very happy to be back as you can imagine," she wrote to one of the Gen. "It doesn't mean I was unhappy in England. No, but as you know we are happy to do the will of God and all these things that happened are part of his plan of love."

She had a different style to Pina. She was a leader, but she knew her own limitations and that everything depended on having the presence of God among them. Together with the others they would build the focolare.

One of her first weekends back, was designated as a weekend of rest. Juanita woke early and went off to do the shopping. Lieta left a note on the kitchen table. "I thought we could do a little tidy up of the garage," she wrote. Margaret and Mary Francis were not impressed. This was not their idea of a relaxing weekend! But what mattered, they remembered, was to love, and so with Lieta they threw themselves into cleaning out the garage and it turned out to be a rest of a different kind.

On Thursday nights they had their 'focolare' night, where they would share about how they were managing or otherwise to live the spirituality in their everyday lives. At the end, Lieta would say "I think that Jesus is present among us". "It was pure magic," recalls Margaret. "She said it with such simplicity. It was everything."

Lieta herself felt that the other focolarine were putting everything into "doubling the love" in the focolare. With each one she had a personal chat, declaring her unity so that they would bring everything ahead together. Little by little she was able to find the balance - finding a real relationship with Jesus in her heart, and finding a relationship with the people around her.

Whenever she was unsure about something, she immediately asked for help from Mari in London. One weekend each month, she travelled to London to meet Mari and the other community leaders to gain from their experience and the light of their support. Pina was visiting Dublin every few months and this too was a tremendous help to Lieta as she found her feet in the new reality.

From November 1982, they were living in the new

focolare centre in Milltown. Before, they had lived in a rented furnished house. When they moved they had to buy furniture. At the beginning they slept on camp beds. Neither Juanita nor Lieta was working, so paying the mortgage and all the bills was quite a challenge. But providence was never lacking in the Dublin focolare.

"We could tell the whole world that God is a Father and the communion of goods a reality among the Christians of today. (....) We asked Jesus for providence and each day it arrived," Lieta wrote. "We sold clothes in second hand shops, books, Centro Ave sacred art, we received Christmas goodies....."
An immediate priority was to get work. Lieta had left a good job in a reputable solicitor's office to go to London, but in spite of this experience, it was hard for her to find work on her return to Dublin, and Juanita was finding it hard too. At the time, 147,000 people were unemployed in Ireland. Each week they joined a long "dole" queue as they lined up to receive the payment for the unemployed. It was a depressing situation.

Looking at the long line of mostly young people, eyes downcast, some reading papers, Lieta thought of Jesus on the cross when He cried out "Why?" He too felt useless and rejected. Suddenly that line up had a new appeal. "It is a deep experience of trying, in a downcast environment like the dole queue, to love all those people who have to take money from the state because they have no work," she wrote.

While she was out of work, Lieta spent much of her time in the focolare with Margaret and they built up a good unity among them. They tried to work together and anticipate each other's needs and became very close. At a certain point, Lieta had a chat with Margaret and pointed out that the life of unity of the Focolare is always concentrated on unity but it must always be a unity that is open. So it was not just "two" of them keeping unity but they had to be open to building that unity with many others. After two months Lieta got a job in a solicitor's office in Capel Street. She was delighted because she felt it was God's will to work, to earn money and to be out in the world with other people.

As time passed, Lieta gradually acclimatised to leading the focolare community. She had an "exquisite" love for each of the three women she lived with. At one stage, Margaret was meant to accompany a group to an international meeting in Rome, but as Lieta thought about it, she felt that Mary Frances should go instead. With great delicacy she asked Margaret would she mind if Mary Frances went in her place. And even though the preparations were well on, Margaret felt such love in the way Lieta was asking her, that she was immediately able to give up the idea of going.

It was this great love that made it easy to confide in Lieta, even when trials came. She was completely open to people, with no judgment, just love. Juanita who lived with her in the Focolare community for many years, recalls a time when she was passing through a difficult moment. Lieta came to her and opened up a conversation. She told her she really wanted to help. And then also declared the measure of love found in the new commandment that they were trying to live in their community: "I'm ready to give my life for you." Juanita experienced such a depth of sisterly love in this declaration, that she felt the difficulty had vanished.

Another time, Margaret approached Lieta. She had become attracted to a man in the community, and one night opened up about it to Lieta. "I was able to tell her absolutely everything," she recalls. Lieta told her not to give in to discouragement. "It happens to us all," she said. "At that moment, a light came in the semi darkness. It was a blinding light which went through me, and a joy and a peace," said Margaret.

Some years later, before she moved to a different focolare centre, Margaret was with Lieta in the kitchen preparing a meal. Lieta turned to her and reminded her of the incident, "because of your openness, you helped me to be open in a similar situation with Mari". "For me it was the fulfilment of that 'I in you and you in me' of the Gospel," said Margaret.

As time passed, Lieta became a big sister to each one, just as Pina had been a mother to her. But she kept her own character and spontaneity. If it was a fine day and they had nothing specific planned, she would immediately propose dropping everything, throwing a few things in the boot of the car and heading off to the beach or the mountains. She liked to seize the moment.

After six months, as she looked back on all the changes, she could see that every loss had been a gain. Mary, who stood beside Jesus at the cross, had been her mother and teacher. She was learning like her, to live with Jesus alone, without leaning on anything or on any person and she was experiencing "the resurrection".

Chapter 8

Fire and Conquest

Time passed, and Lieta also grew into her role of being the co- director of the Focolare movement. By now the men's focolare was well established, led by Bruno Carrera from Italy, a man seven years her senior. Together they oversaw the growth of the movement with all its branches - New Youth: catering for the young people, New Humanity: for those drawn to bring the Christian revolution into society, New Parishes: for priests and parish collaborators, New Families: for couples and children. There were also movements for priests, religious and sisters.

Bruno had worked alongside Pina for many years, so it took time for him to adjust to Lieta's style of leadership. They had different approaches. Lieta was more fiery and sometimes this led to disagreements. She expected more from people, while Bruno was more gentle. She was more leading, wanting to organise lots of activities for the community; he liked a more paced approach. Each week they met to plan events and discuss matters to do with the movement and gradually they got to know each other well. After a period there was, in Bruno's words "a beautiful unity".

Meanwhile Lieta was still working full time. It was

not easy to come home from a long day's work and set into organising activities, meeting people, writing letters or even cleaning the house. After a period, she realised she needed to reduce her working hours so as to be at home more for people and for the activities of the movement. The pace of life was intense and even simple things were being overlooked. They were all tired, she realised, and had to do less.

What was important was to do what God wanted, even if this meant saying no to people who asked them to go and speak about the movement. "Ireland is more alive than ever to this Gospel spirituality and everyone is asking for us," she wrote. But she understood that the movement was not something merely human. God had his own plan for it. "Maybe God wants us to show that the movement is something divine and not human or to our measure."

Still she dreamt of part time work...and having discussed the matter with Mari, took the courageous decision of giving up her full time job. Unemployment was still very high in Ireland and walking into her house one day, she wondered how she would ever get part time work when so many Irish people were unemployed.

One Wednesday she went to sign on for the dole in the hope that she would receive some unemployment assistance but the official explained to her that she was not entitled to any unemployment pay as she was only looking for part time work. Despondently she turned and left.

She was scared because she knew it was almost impossible to find part time employment. But God was her Father and so with an act of faith, she entrusted the situation to Him, even though she could not see any possibilities. "I believed in his love and I asked him to look after it," she wrote to a friend.

Returning to her home that same day, the telephone rang. It was Marian Gilligan telling her that a part time job had arisen at the school where she worked, and she had set up an interview for Lieta with the headmistress. It was God's answer. A week later, Lieta was back at work, this time in a busy second-ary girl's school. It was just a five minutes drive from the focolare centre.

Marian was also working at the school. She had muscular dystrophy and was just reaching the point of needing to use a wheelchair at school, something she was loath to do. Lieta encouraged her. She would carry her books to the car each day, and fold up the wheelchair. They could do it togeth-er. Suddenly the change was not so daunting and with Lieta's support, Marian took the decision and started using the wheelchair each day.

There were two of them in the school. Jesus said

"Where two or more are gathered in my name, I am there." Immediately Lieta saw the chance for something wonderful at Notre Dame Secondary school. She and Marian could have the presence of Jesus among them each day. Conscious of this she worked diligently at the office administration, and did not miss a chance to get to know the girls one by one, and the teachers.

One day a teacher came into the office. Lieta was alone working away. The teacher, who did not have a religious faith, was about to go on maternity leave. Lieta could see she was worried about the birth. She had a good relationship with the teacher and stopping her work, told her warmly that she would pray that everything would go well. "She lit up and before leaving she reminded me to remember her," Lieta wrote to a friend.

After a while, Lieta and Marian started a Word of Life[9] meeting in the school, where each week they shared how they were trying to put the Gospel into practice in their day to day lives with a group of 15 year old girls.

In 1985 seventy young people set off to a Focolare youth festival in Rome. It was a very exciting moment and everyone was very enthusiastic. In the midst of the excitement, Lieta was suddenly beset by a private inner storm. She was having unexpected temptations, in particular against the virtue of purity. At that time she happened to be reading the

[9] Word of Life - A sentence from Scripture that the members of the Movement strive to put into practice each month.

life of Maximilian Kolbe and decided to follow his example and put herself into the hands of Mary Immaculate in whom she found support and consolation.

She confided the temptations to a close friend and her own determination, out of love for the people around her, to choose Jesus forsaken in that suffering too. When He cried out 'Why?' on the cross, He felt a sinner as well. He was the King of her life. "I don't want to have either creatures or things in my soul," she wrote. She only wanted to be in the present moment doing what God wanted. "I know that in this way I am completely free and always ready to love the others and not myself."

After a period the trial passed and she experienced a new interior freedom. She was not afraid to face anyone - from the least person to Church or state personalities, because she wrote, "I am convinced that this Gospel spirituality is everything".

Chiara Lubich, the founder of Focolare, had never visited Ireland, except for a short touchdown in Shannon airport many years earlier en route to New York. But in 1986 word came through that she might visit Ireland later that year.

Lieta, Juanita, Mary Francis, Ita and Therese, living in the focolare centre, felt it would be a great opportunity for each person to get to know Chiara in a personal way. Everyone was thrilled at this great news and the movement went into overdrive. Lieta felt the best preparation she could make was to live the Gospel more intensely, even in the simplest acts of her day.

One day for example, they were living the Word of Life: "Whoever doesn't put aside his own life...cannot be my disciple". That morning Lieta put the two bikes outside the front of the house for Juanita and Mary Francis. But Mary Frances ended up taking the bus and her bike was left in the front garden. Lieta spotted it. First she thought of just leaving it behind the door at the side of the house which lead to the back garden. But inside her a voice told her: "If it rains, the bike will be ruined". She remembered the word of life. "This was something very small in comparison to my life. So I brought the bike inside," she wrote. "That act of love, done for Jesus in the morning put a stamp on the whole day."

In the end, Chiara did not visit Ireland in 1986. She fell ill and the trip to the US, Britain and Ireland was cancelled, but she did send Dori Zambone, one of her first companions, to address a large gathering of friends and members of the Focolare at the ALSA hall in Dublin in November that year.

Shortly after, Lieta said goodbye to three of the women she was living with in the focolare, as Mary Francis left to work in Rome, Ita, an Irish focolarina set off to teach in the Cameroons, Africa, and Therese from France, left to join the focolare community in New Zealand. Together they had built the unity in the focolare so that Jesus was always present.

It had been a special period, Lieta wrote. "where God helped us to see each other new and unity was complete".

Chapter 9

Storms

The following years were hard ones. As the movement grew, and Lieta matured, she had to face all sorts of trials. A young woman living with her went through a period of complete darkness and moved out. Lieta tried to accept this new situation but it was difficult, especially as now there were only three of them living in the focolare centre.

She was helped by the others, Juanita and Vania, a focolarina from Hong Kong, who had just arrived in Ireland. They tried to share all the difficulties and to listen to each other right to the end. "This is what happened recently with Vania," Lieta wrote. "I stopped and we talked and we said everything we felt. Together we understood that Jesus was asking us to love Him by being alone with Him, loving with our will and not just when it is beautiful. It only took a few minutes to have the fullness of His presence among us once again just like we do on the most beautiful days."

Little by little Lieta understood that she could not do everything herself. She knew she always tried to give everything, but at a certain point she had to let others help too. "I must learn to trust others more," she wrote. She realised that her focolare was not just the women that she was living with, but all the pillars of the movement - the Volunteers[10], Gen, religious sisters and married focolarine[11]. It was together with all these people that she would lead the movement.

At times there were difficulties which she could not share with anyone. "At this point I remember the choice I've made of wanting only Jesus and I want to remain faithful to him right to the end," she wrote to Mari. She had a very strong relationship of trust with Mari in London, whom she visited each month for the meeting of the zone council. England was a solid and well established zone in Focolare terms and most of the emphasis of these meetings was on the movement there. Ireland was a different world and often came in for scant mention. Lieta learned to lose her thoughts, plans and projections for her adopted country so as to give her contribution to the development of the whole zone.

One day on the flight to London, she met a smartly dressed young woman from Argentina. She was married and living in London. A woman of the world, her life revolved around material possessions. She had no belief in God. Lieta chatted to her for the duration of the journey and they agreed to keep in touch. Later the woman rang her in Dublin. Her brother was in Dublin, lost and without money. Lieta arranged to meet him to give him some.

---

[10] Volunteers of God - lay men and women committed to bringing God into every corner of society

[11] Married focolarine - female members of the small core communities of the Focolare who while married, also consecrate themselves to God and live for the ideal of unity.

During a long telephone conversation, the woman asked her why she was in Dublin and Lieta explained her life choice. There was a deep communion of soul between them, and the woman explained she was getting divorced from her husband and asked Lieta to visit her. She said she would. What was of most importance to Lieta was the person beside her 'now'. In each person, she met another Jesus.

One autumn day around this time, she and the others were preparing to go out for a long walk. They were tired and looking forward to the break. Then the doorbell rang. It was a priest from Northern Ireland with two girls from his parish. The three of them were very low in themselves, seeing everything black. Immediately Lieta, Juanita, Vania and Paula (an Irish woman who had recently moved into the focolare centre) let go of all their plans for a relaxing walk and started talking to them.

"Then little by little, it seemed that the morning light entered and the light became so strong that they were all changed," Lieta wrote later to Mari. "We spoke to them of the real aim of the movement which is not to make us feel comfy, but to draw close to those without God." When they left they were happy. "Afterwards there was a beautiful Spencer Tracy film on about the life of Einstein, and we managed to have a rest too!"

Often at Christmas time, she and the other focolarine travelled to the Mariapolis centre north of

London at Welwyn Garden City. It was usually a great joy to be together, with time for swapping stories, sport, rest, games, impromptu concerts and long chats over the dinner table as the thirty or so women caught up on each other's lives.

For Christmas 1987, Lieta, Paula and Vania went to Welwyn. But Lieta was not her usual happy self. She was, as Paula said, "absent".

It was as if she needed to find independence in a different way, almost as if the recent years had seen a maturation, not only in herself, but in the people entrusted to her and this was urging Lieta to find a new expression more true to the changed circumstances.

One day a few of them, including Lieta and Paula went to play badminton. Lieta's competitive spirit rose to the fore. She played to win. But she was not happy: the more she thought of herself and was determined to do her own thing, the unhappier she was. Later they all got together for a moment of sharing. Spontaneously different people spoke and then taking a deep breath, Lieta opened up and explained how she had been upset but had realised that "God loves me as I am". It was clear this was something very deep for her as she began to cry.

A month later in Rome at her annual retreat, Lieta listened to a talk about Mary. She understood that all she was experiencing was part of God's plan. She was following Mary's footsteps. Suddenly she saw everything in a new light and felt "a new creature". Back in Dublin, Lieta continued to live through a difficult time. Many close members of the movement were sick, as was Lieta's own mother. Her aunt had recently died and two new members of her focolare community had moved out to live alone. Lieta felt a little sick herself "and not only physically," she wrote.

In the divine economy, suffering is always fruitful, and the summer Mariapolis (summer gathering) of 1988 was an exceptional one. One person described it as "the most beautiful and strongest Mariapolis we have ever had, where many experienced deeply the presence of Mary and committed themselves to taking her home and to re-living her".

Lieta gave a talk about Mary and it flowed out of her. She was a living witness to the words she was speaking. Bruno remarked, "I felt Mary had taken over [the Mariapolis]. It was like a new changeover in the life of the movement in Ireland."

Chapter 10

Preparing people for Paradise

Very early on a cold January day in 1989, Lieta was woken up by the phone. She heard the devastating news that Ita Lyng, the Irish focolarina with whom she had lived for a few years, had died. She had caught malaria in Fontem, Africa, and within a few days was dead.

Lieta had to break the news to Ita's parents. She called Fr Brendan Purcell, and together they travelled to Dun Laoghaire to tell them the heartbreaking news. On the way Lieta thought of Ita's life.

Ita had made a radical choice of God almost from her first meeting with the movement while studying in University College Dublin in the early 70s. There she went to a Word of Life group 'as an observer' with her cousin Marian Gilligan. The sentence the students were trying to live was "Whatever you do to the least you do to me." The next day, while waiting for her bus to college, she saw a little girl across the road with a bottle of milk in her hand. The child dropped the bottle and burst into tears. The bus was arriving. Ita remembered the Word of Life and in that moment made her choice. Letting the bus go, she went across to the little girl, bought her a fresh bottle of milk and in her own words passed from being an 'observer', to being an 'activist'. That night she went home on foot as she had spent her bus fare on the milk and understood that in order to love the way Jesus loves, you had to pay in the first person.

A few years later she had made her choice to give herself to God completely in the focolare. She had lived with Lieta and was never sick. Early in 1987 she had moved to live and work in the little focolare town of Fontem in the Cameroons.

At 8.30am that morning, Lieta and Fr Brendan stood at the door of Tommy and Ita Lyng's house and told them the terrible news. The couple immediately left for their daughter's funeral in Fontem on the west coast of Africa.

The focolare community in Ireland was shocked by the news that Ita had died. Everyone had loved her - her good humour and simplicity, her strong determination once she took a decision, her constant willingness to write and perform comic sketches taking off 'the old self' of our selfish ways before we've been struck by the Gospel. When her parents, Tommy and Ita returned from Fontem with a video of Ita's funeral, the community gathered in a large hall to look at it and collectively mourn their wonderful departed friend.

Ita's departure put everyone in front of God, none more so than Lieta. If Ita could go so quickly, so could each one. And would they be ready? "We too want to accomplish the plan God has for us with the same faithfulness," Lieta wrote.

Meditating on Ita's death, she realised that the movement was not just about trying to build a better world through unity between people, but it was to "send people to Paradise". In the past she had feared death but now, with this new understanding, she was happy to do everything she could to accompany people to the doors of heaven.

Among these was a niece of Ita's, Edel Byrne, a twelve year old girl with Spina Bifida who was gravely ill at the time. Edel was a girl of extraordinary strength and truth. Although she could do little physically, as a young child she felt the responsibility of the Gen 4[12] and when she was older, for the Gen 3, regularly praying the rosary for them.

Lieta developed a very special relationship with Edel, visiting her and taking her out on occasional trips. Four months before she went to Paradise (aged 13), Lieta arranged for her to meet Focolare founder, Chiara Lubich, who gave her a new name 'Luce' (Light) explaining to her that the more she lived each moment as if it were her last, the more the light would grow in her. Edel had been passing a moment of darkness, but these words become her touchstone.

And in Lieta, the conviction grew that the Holy Journey was "the most important thing".

---

[12] Gen 4 - Branch of Focolare for young children, Gen 3 - Branch for older children

Chapter 11

Going 'native' at Magheramore

October 1990, and Lieta and Bruno sat at a large conference table at the Focolare movement's head-quarters in Rome. Chiara was at the top of the table and together they were discussing the development of the movement in the UK and Ireland. When it came to Ireland's turn, Chiara said she thought the time was right for the country no longer to be linked to the UK, but to be a separate zone in its own right. It was a sign of how the movement had matured and developed: it was now ready to stand alone. Lieta was absolutely overjoyed. At the end of the meeting, she spontaneously jumped up, ran to Chiara and gave her two kisses on each cheek.

Back in Ireland the news was greeted with raptur-ous applause at the update on the Delegates' Meeting a few weeks later. By now the movement was a well articulated body with members spread geographically to the main cities outside of Dublin and communities in Belfast, Strabane, Kilkenny, Dungarvan, Ballinasloe, Clonmel and Cork. The Word of Life was being translated into Irish.

The life of the Gospel that the members of the move-ment were trying to live began to be expressed in social actions. The youth branch, then known as 'New Youth,' ran a weekly coffee and entertainment cafe in Rathgar for students who were often isolated in Dublin's 'flatland'. They were also involved in projects with the travelling community, the disabled and a youth club in Cabra. Together with adult members of the movement, they worked together on projects, like the campaign to insert a pro life amendment in Ireland's constitution.

New Humanity[13] was involved in a variety of actions: fundraising for earthquake victims in Panama and promoting peace in the Lebanon through a series of visits to the embassies of Egypt, Iran, Russia and the US. As the movement developed so did its need for a permanent base for the continuous activities of the branches: Ireland needed a Mariapolis Centre[14].

Lieta and Bruno returned from Rome and almost immediately signed a lease on what was to be Ireland's first Mariapolis centre in County Wicklow. Located in an area called Magheramore on the coast, south of Wicklow town, the small centre had originally been stables near a large Georgian mansion which now acted as the headquarters of the Columban Sisters. A beautiful avenue covered in huge rhododendron bushes led into a walled courtyard, with two sides made up of the renovated stable buildings, the other two by old high stone walls. A pathway led to the main house, and past this, down a private pedestrian way to a small cove, Magheramore beach. It was idyllic.

---

[13] New Humanity, the branch for Focolare members eager to bring the Gospel into every area of society.

[14] Cf. Footnote 3.

The rustic buildings struck a chord with Lieta. She felt at home there, almost as if she was back in Argentina. When she went to Magheramore, she went 'native', wearing her poncho and mountain boots, with her socks up over her trousers. She and the other focolarine would collect firewood and light a fire in a half barrel. Lieta cooked 'assados' [Argentinean barbequed steak] in the courtyard. "It was back to nature, total relax," recalls Paula.

The new Mariapolis Centre was in an idyllic location and though it was limited in space, it was a wonderful setting where the members of the Focolare Movement could organise courses and all kinds of events to deepen their understanding of the spirituality and introduce it to other people. It had one large meeting room, which also served as a dining room. At the entrance was a large reception area leading into a kitchen and eleven bedrooms catering for about 30 people. The centre straightaway felt like home, and setting up the dining area at the end of each meeting became a game.

Writing to Chiara in November 1990, you could sense Lieta's joy at this new stage in the development of the movement in Ireland. "In my soul I have a huge gratitude to God for calling me one day to the focolare... I have asked Jesus during these days to take complete possession of me and I give myself once again and completely to Him so as to be an instrument of unity."

There was a lot of work to be done. Over the Christmas holidays Lieta and the focolarine were joined by members of the community who dropped in to paint, hammer and sew. Providence arrived from all corners. A woman working for a major company in Dublin noticed they were throwing out a set of 70 office chairs as they were re-decorating. She asked could she have them. Days later, the chairs were stacked ready for use in Magheramore. Portable partitions arrived to separate the dining area in the main hall.

With the others, Lieta prayed, worked and rested. Describing Christmas in a letter she wrote: "It was very beautiful for us and also for the Gen, volunteers and some new families who were with us or who came for a day to visit and work at the centre." One day she gathered with some of the women closest to her to plan the year ahead. Looking at all the work to be done, for a moment she felt almost discouraged. How could they, with their limited strength, reach everyone and manage everything? But then she remembered that they had not chosen to build an organisation, but to love Jesus on the cross in his "why?" and then to try to love everyone. Then "the Holy Spirit tells us what the will of God is in the present giving us the light, strength and time. He works miracles that are often tangible," she wrote.

In the years that followed, the movement continued its development. The 1990s were a charismatic time as Chiara launched initiative after initiative in the field of economics, international relations, education and health. Lieta was awestruck by the imagination of God who was bringing about such marvels in the mosaic which was the Focolare Movement.

And not just in faraway places like Brazil, but in Ireland too. Two new focolare centres opened in Dublin: a men's centre in Harold's Cross and a women's centre in Templeogue. In addition, family focolares (made up of couples who were both married focolarini) offered to move with their families to places where there was a demand for a presence of the movement. A number of businesses based on the newly launched "Economy of Communion"[15] came to life, and large scale gatherings, like the concert of the international band 'Gen Verde' at the Point in Dublin brought the movement into the public eye. The weight of responsibility for the movement was firmly on Lieta and Bruno's shoulders, but even with this, she always managed to focus on people and practical service.

One day she heard that a recently bereaved Volunteer[16] could not go to her congress in Rome as she did not want to leave her daughter, Marian Gilligan, who had muscular dystrophy, on her own. Lieta's solution was a practical one, she and Paola would move into the house and stay with Marian.

---

[15] Economy of Communion - a system of economics where businesses operate in the market place and divide their profits in three parts: one to assist those in need, another to develop structures that promote the 'culture of giving' and a third for the expenses and growth of the firm.

[16] Cf Footnote 12

It was a very special time. Marian was teaching and would leave for school each day. Lieta stayed in the house, cooking and cleaning. "Nothing was too much trouble for her," said Marian. They lived a very simple life, but full of joy and happiness. "Lieta liked to have a good laugh, relax and have fun. Yet always she had a deep, practical love for everyone and a big heart," recalls Marian.

In September 1994, Dick, the father of one of the married focolarine, lay dying in hospital. A very good friend of the family was at home looking after their one year old son as she and her husband kept vigil by Dick's bedside. But Susan knew that the lady would love to be there with Dick as well. She racked her brain trying to think of who she could ask to take over minding their son. Maybe Lieta could suggest someone she could ask, she thought as she rang her.

Lieta's reply was immediate. "I'm on my way. Tell Joan to get ready to go. I'll look after the baby. Don't worry about coming back. Stay as long as you need at the hospital with your Dad."

Minutes later, she was at their home, and there she stayed for hours and hours, playing with the baby, feeding him and putting him to bed. She was still there waiting as they returned hours later from the hospital having seen Dick off to the gates of Paradise.

Coming up to Easter another year, Lieta talked to Mary, another married focolarina. Her husband had been building their house for some years, and they had been living with her mother in law. She had young children and longed to be in her own home. She was at the end of her tether and crying. Lieta listened. "Can we help you?"

The house needs to be painted, said Mary. "We'll come and make a start on it," was Lieta's immediate offer. On Good Friday she and some of the other focolarine arrived at the new house and set to painting the kitchen. They were all filled with Easter joy as they worked. At a certain point they stopped to go to the Passion service and Holy Communion. Lieta's hands were covered in paint. She quickly concealed them with gloves.

Marian, a leader among the Volunteer women, recalls the time her father was very ill in hospital having just had a major heart attack. He was a fit man and only 64. The whole family was absolutely devastated as he had always appeared to be so healthy. She was in touch with Lieta by phone telling her about her Dad's progress. Without saying anything, Lieta decided to go to the hospital to support her.

That day was a real low point for Marian. She thought her father was not going to make it and went into the chapel to unburden herself to Jesus, crying her heart out. As she came out of the chapel there was Lieta waiting for her, a smile on her face. It was just the right moment. Lieta gave her a big hug, and then they exchanged a few heartfelt words. With her support, Marian was ready to get back on track and be love for her family and a support for her mum.

It was this capacity of not fearing suffering, of running towards people in difficulty and offering concrete support, that endeared Lieta to so many people. She did not fear taking tough decisions - advising a family to take a strong course of action against a wayward son, begging a pregnant girl not to have an abortion and offering to take the baby herself, telling a panic stricken young woman to take on the responsibility of looking after her invalid father.

When she was not sure of her own capacity to solve a problem, she had the humility to call in help. One time one of the Volunteers began to be attracted by New Age philosophies and the idea of reincarnation. Lieta listened to her with complete detachment, and then after a while suggested that she write to Chiara for advice. She understood that her friend's questions were not just prompted by curiosity but a deep desire to know the Truth and to help her friends. "Why don't I come to see you one day with a priest, and we can talk about these things with Jesus in our midst?" she suggested.

A few days later, Lieta and a priest friend made the visit. They talked. Lieta remained in silence, a transparent nothingness so that Jesus would really be present among them. When the priest spoke, he said he felt it was the 'Word of Jesus' speaking, and "that impacted".

As they left, Lieta gave her friend a beautifully framed picture of Jesus forsaken along with the meditation, 'I have only one Spouse'. Her friend felt loved and understood, but also satisfied with the explanations she had received which she felt had come from God.

Chapter 13

Links to Home

Lieta lived most of her life in Ireland, becoming an Irish citizen and even doing a course in the Irish language. Yet she always kept a strong link with her family and homeland, visiting Argentina every few years, and in particular in the late 80s and 90s as her parents became old and frail. Generous by nature, she went armed to Argentina with presents for everyone - her immediate family - parents, brothers and sisters, and her many nieces and nephews. Although she did not see them very often, she managed to keep a personal bond with each one. She had an intense love for her family and tried to be totally involved in their decisions and traumas. In 1988 one such drama unfolded while she was home for Easter.

By then her parents Tiburcio and Carmen were alone in the large family home in La Plata. They were both getting on in years, and Lieta's Mum suffered from claustrophobia. Like many people who have had to struggle to get by, Carmen had become a great hoarder, holding onto things that she thought might be useful "at some stage".

"It was a disaster," recalls Neldi. "She was surrounded by an accumulation of many things and we said

'This isn't good for her.'" The doctor advised a change. Together the family, with Tiburcio's agreement, plotted a move to another, smaller house with a nice back garden. It was the right moment.

In the midst of the brewing family trauma, Lieta arrived from Ireland to celebrate Easter, laden with a huge box of chocolates. But tension was in the air as the time had come to break the news to their Mum that she and Tiburcio were to move. Tiburcio had agreed, although he would not say so in front of Carmen, as she had always been the one to rule the roost.

Over dinner one day, they began to discuss the change. Lieta had an enormous love for her mother. They explained the situation to her. The house was too big, too cluttered, too much work. Carmen's own doctor had recommended that she and Tiburcio move to a smaller house. The family had found a lovely house, suitable to their needs. They would look after the move. All would be well, and in the end they would be a lot more comfy and happy. Carmen was devastated, her head bent low, with the expression of a "sacrificial victim" on her face. "But you want to kill me! This will break my heart. I cannot leave that house," she cried.

Lieta sat in silence listening to her Mum. She was very upset too. She had never had to be tough with a parent like that. It seemed so terrible. But with her brothers and sisters she remained steadfast. In her heart however she was not at peace. Was it really the right thing to give her mother this enormous suffering at her age?

A few days later she rang Neldi in Cordoba and told her how she was feeling and her questions. Neldi reiterated that they were doing it on the doctor's advice and she was not prepared to change her mind. In the end, Lieta was convinced.

Shortly after, Tiburcio and Carmen moved house. As promised, the Betoño sons did a big de-clutter on the old family home, clearing out the accumulation of a lifetime, and taking just what was needed to the new house. Carmen still reproached the family and Lieta for their decision, but gradually she settled down and the unity in the family was once again restored.

Three years later in 1991 Carmen became very ill, and Lieta returned to Argentina. She saw how her mother had grown spiritually through the illness, accepting everything from God. "She [my mother] is ready for what Jesus may ask of her and offers everything for the movement," she wrote on her return to Ireland. Seeing her Mum so at peace in the midst of her suffering, convinced Lieta that God is truly Love for each person.

However Carmen's health got worse. In 1993 she had a heart attack and for a year lived without being able to speak in a semi-conscious state. The strong, independent mother was reduced to a passive, immobile patient, lying on a bed.

In January 1994, Lieta travelled again to Argentina, and spent a month near her mother's bedside. It was heartbreaking for her to see her beloved mother, going from a vibrant and strong character to being completely uncommunicative. Lieta saw her as a little saint, living the last period of her life as she had lived before, "completely up[17] , in the will of God, smiling at everyone and allowing herself to be cared for like a little lamb", she wrote.

When she left her mother to return to Dublin, she waited for her to fall asleep to give her a final kiss because since her mother could not communicate, Lieta did not know whether she should tell her that she was leaving and that perhaps they would not see each other again. She felt herself it was the last time she would see her mother, but it was too hard to say it. In the end her farewell was a kiss. In turmoil she left to return to Ireland.

In the following months, Carmen became more lucid, and her brothers asked her to come back to Argentina, but in Lieta's own words, she did not have "the strength to see her in that condition again and to have to leave her once more," and so "subconsciously" she made various excuses.

Then on the last day of the year in 1994, Carmen died. Lieta was filled with regret. She grieved for her mother, but in addition she felt the pain of reproach. "I should have gone to see her again, it would have given her joy," she thought.

---

[17] 'completely up' - by this Lieta means spiritually at the summit.

Her reproach to herself was a new face of her spouse, Jesus, crying out "why?" on the cross, and she said a new 'yes' to Him and tried to be happy believing firmly that "all that God wills or permits is for our sanctification". Every time the regret returned, she asked Jesus "for the hundredfold of paradise for my mother".

A month after her Mum's death, Lieta returned to Argentina. Her Dad was now living with her older sister Cecilia and her family, who saw his presence with them as "a gift". "They love him a lot," Lieta wrote to a friend.

Then she set off for the Focolare's little town O'Higgins where her mother had been buried. Standing by her grave she experienced that her mother was present more than ever because of the reality that Jesus himself was present among them. In 1998, Lieta returned to Argentina, this time to accompany her father to heaven. For eighteen days he was in hospital, gradually growing weaker, but somehow managing to forge strong bonds of love and communion with his eight children and the hospital staff. This time Lieta was in time to say goodbye, arriving three days before his 'flight'.

Sitting at his bedside with her sisters and brothers, she contemplated God's plan on her wonderful father, the 'just man', as she wrote afterwards. On 18th May he died after "a race of love to the end. Already we feel the atmosphere of heaven", Lieta,

Neldi, Mercedes and Renatina wrote in a note to Chiara. A day later they solemnly took him to be buried with their mother at the Mariapolis O'Higgins.

Lieta was not to return to Argentina for another four years. Her next visit would be much, much longer, and this time she would be the person at the centre of the family's concern.

Chapter 14

Construction

1996: The Focolare Movement was going ahead on all fronts. There were four focolare centres in Dublin and for the first time, a 'foothold' focolare had been established in Belfast. This presence in Belfast created a sense of deep peace in the community even when the IRA ceasefire collapsed later in the year.

In January Lieta was at home in the zone centre in Dublin. Chiara was to visit London in November, and a niggling hope was stirring that she might come a little further.... to Ireland. While Lieta oversaw renovations to the kitchen and an attic extension, she dreamt of Chiara in Ireland. A little time later she heard that Chiara would only go to London, but Lieta pressed ahead, as if she was coming. She would still do the renovations for her, just in case.

Providence arrived little by little for the kitchen, the bathroom, the windows, for an attic conversion, and to build office storage to house all the documentation for the movement. Juanita and Maria, a German focolarina, left each day for work. Lieta stayed at home to supervise the renovations. It was a real test of patience with workmen promising to come, and not turning up, and a test of endurance - the noise and the dust when they did come! Mistakes were made. She tried to be tough to ensure the work was done properly, and at the same time be her usual gentle, loving self. It was not easy. Many days, Lieta was tearing her hair out with frustration. It took five months for the work to be completed.

Elsewhere around the world, what was coming to life was the birth of a number of 'little towns of witness'. Many grew up around Mariapolis centres. Lieta and Bruno had asked Chiara about the possibility of a little town for Ireland in 1992 but she had advised caution - multiply the focolare centres first, before thinking of a 'little town'.

The movement was still renting the small Mariapolis centre in Magheramore on a year to year basis, but by now it was too small for its needs. Lieta and Bruno, together with all the members of the movement were on the lookout for a property they could buy as a true home for the movement. 'Operation Brick' came to life, where people committed themselves to pay for one or more bricks of the future Mariapolis centre.

Over the years many religious men and women had come in touch with Focolare in Ireland. Some were selling land, or old convents. Through the grapevine, Lieta and Bruno started to hear of properties that were vacant or about to come on the market, and the visits to these began.

The general day-to-day activities of the movement were going ahead but Lieta and Bruno felt it was the moment of God for Ireland to have its own Mariapolis Centre, and hopefully 'little town' too. At times Lieta felt dissatisfied because things did not go ahead the way she wanted. In a letter she complained about "obstacles, indecisive and tired people" but then she reminded herself of her choice of Jesus in his abandonment as "my only good for all my life". Thinking of Him, she found life again and unity with everyone. She was convinced the movement was God's work and not theirs.

In September, before she and Bruno left for the annual delegates' meeting in Rome, they heard of a property for sale in Maynooth. Their hopes were raised. The university town with a population of around 9,000, is 24 kilometres west of Dublin, with train and bus links to the city. It has the national seminary, and is seen as the heart of the Catholic Church in Ireland.

The Salesian Fathers were selling a large modern property on campus. It had 55 bedrooms, a chapel and dining facilities. But there was no hall. In addition, there were no private grounds, although it was surrounded by the green open space of the college campus.   Could this be the building God had planned as Ireland's first permanent Mariapolis Centre?

Lieta was full of excitement. Together with Bruno they discussed it with Chiara and the centre of the movement at the September meeting. In a way circumstances would decide - including the cost and whether the money could be raised. In the meantime, a commitment to an earlier possible purchaser kept everyone in suspense. The Salesians asked the Focolare to wait - they were not sure if the property was available for purchase or not. Lieta was detached: "We are happy to wait longer and to have a final answer from the Salesians and at the same time we are ready to start looking for another centre," she wrote.

A few months later, another property on the same campus went up for sale. It was even bigger. Maybe they could use it for an Economy of Communion Language school? Lieta's mind was in overdrive as she pondered all the possibilities. Believing in Providence and the love of God, she and Bruno made an offer. It was not accepted. As 1996 came to a close they were back to square one.

Lieta was not dismayed. It was a question of persevering, she thought. "We are happy because everything has a purpose. Nothing is in vain," she wrote. "Our life becomes simple, without worries. It is enough that we are turned towards the Father."

But the Father was not going to just drop a Mariapolis Centre in their lap. Lieta knew they had to do their part to bring about His plan and that meant investigating buildings, land, properties. She became like a private investigator on a mission. At first they looked at convents and large houses, then after a while they thought of buying a green field site and building, so it was trips to open fields and landscapes.

"Not a day passes when we don't look at a piece of land or a building. We feel that the eternal Father will intervene at the right moment, because humanly speaking the prices of property are going up each day but we have trust that we will find what we are looking for," she wrote. Her day-to-day diary attested to the many trips she made: to Blackrock, Swords and Balbriggan in Dublin, to Maynooth and Kilcock in Kildare, to Bray in Wicklow, to Mornington in Meath. In May with the focolarine, she visited the Marian shrine of Knock, in the West of Ireland to beg Mary for her assistance.

Suddenly the Salesian property came back into the equation again. This time it seemed a real possibility. Lieta and Bruno met a large group of members to decide together how to raise the money. A builder visited the premises with them, then a fire inspector and an engineer. Finally it seemed they had found Ireland's Mariapolis Centre.

With her heart full of high hopes, Lieta set off to the holiday Mariapolis[18] in Roscarberry, West Cork in June. The Mariapolis centre in Maynooth was just a phone call away. While at the Mariapolis, the call

---

[18] Holiday Mariapolis - A weeklong gathering, where members and friends share a holiday together with the presence of Jesus in their midst.

came through, but it was not the call Lieta wanted to hear. The deal was off. She was with Bruno when she got the news and burst into tears.

"It was the only time I saw Lieta cry," recalls Bruno. "We thought we were getting the place from the Salesians and during the Mariapolis we rang the priest and heard the deal was off. For the first time ever I saw Lieta crying. It was heartbreaking for me. I had never experienced it before. I was upset too." But a 'No' was not going to be the end. In her heart Lieta knew that God had a place, a home, for the Focolare Movement in Ireland. They could not give up now. It was just a matter of pressing on with the search. She, Bruno and everyone else, redoubled their efforts.

And then it happened. At the end of the summer, Juanita was surfing the internet and came across an advertisement for the sale of a small country hotel in County Kildare - Curryhillls House. It was an old Georgian mansion with a new block of bedrooms attached and stood on seven acres of land.

Máire O'Byrne, a close friend, who had just moved from Kildare to Dublin to be closer to the focolare centre, offered to take Lieta and Bruno to see the hotel. She had already accompanied Lieta on a number of visits to possible Mariapolis centres, days which she and Lieta thoroughly enjoyed as they weighed up the pros and cons of each property.

They drove through Clane and on out towards Prosperous and turned into the long drive leading to Curryhills House Hotel. As soon as Bruno saw the avenue leading to the Georgian House, Maire says, "he fell in love with it". The owner of the hotel showed them around. Bruno was entranced, Lieta less so. She saw all the practical challenges - the laborious solid fuel heating system, the old electrics, the rambling interior, the kitchen needing modernisation. Instead Bruno saw the avenue, the separation from the world, the beautiful Georgian House with its preservation order and the fine grounds.

The main house had a large bar and a smaller sitting and reception room on the main floor. Below was a dining room, and a discotheque (which could also be used as an overflow dining area). A modern wing at right angles to the old building housed the new bedroom block - ten en suite twin bedrooms. Upstairs in the older building were another four bedrooms, two en suite. Outside were two large car parks, and various barns, one of which contained hundreds of turkeys, being fattened for Christmas.

The property had enormous potential, especially because of its location - outside Dublin, and yet within an hour's drive from the capital. It was just a 15 minutes drive to two main artery motorways, one leading south to Limerick and Cork the other north west to Sligo. At the time both motorways were under construction. Using either of these motorways, the M50 motorway which circled Dublin, could be reached in half an hour. From the point of view of access, Curryhills House was perfectly placed for people coming from any direction in Ireland. God had chosen well.

Lieta tried not to get too excited, but she sensed a plan of God in the discovery of this property, especially as, unlike the one in Maynooth which they had come so close to buying, this had land and the possibility of building.

At the end of September she and Bruno set off for the delegates' meeting in Rome. They had a number of people advising them about the purchase, a Volunteer woman ready to place a booking deposit, an experienced business man happy to donate a portion of the purchase price. "He advised us to put down a deposit if we were interested, and then go to Rome, and that is what we did," recalls Bruno. When Lieta and Bruno met Chiara at the meeting, they showed her pictures of Curryhills House and she immediately exclaimed "But this is a 'little town'!"

Lieta's joy knew no bounds. She kept her heart fixed on Jesus and took the step not to be attached to anything happening, and yet day by day positive answers continued to arrive. She and Bruno made tentative plans. They immediately thought of moving their two focolare centres to the grounds of the new Mariapolis Centre.

"In this way," they wrote to Chiara, "our members, spread around the country, will be able to participate in and live the life of the movement on a regular basis and there will be a beating heart and centre of unity....."

Chiara thought the plan a good one, and it was all systems go. Back in Ireland their solicitor worked hard finalising the deal. He faxed through the contracts. Lieta and Bruno signed them. By the end of the meeting in Rome, everything was signed and sealed. Their perseverance had paid off. They had finally secured a Mariapolis Centre, a permanent home for the movement in Ireland.

Lieta, Bruno and Bishop Laurence Ryan at Mariapolis Radiosa
(Curryhills House), 1998

Lieta at Delegates
meeting, 1995.

Left to right: Lieta,
Chiara, Don Foresi,
Bruno

Lieta at work, painting a fence at Mariapolis
Radiosa, 1999

Lieta and Bruno blow out a candle on a cake at party marking first anniversary of purchase of Mariapolis Radiosa

Close up Lieta

Mariapolis 2001. Left to righ: (front row) Joe McCarroll, Lieta, Bishop Ray Field, Bruno Carrera. Back row: Sarah O'Brien, Chris O'Broin, Anna McHugh, Kate O'Brien

Lieta with her sister Kuqui and her husband Martin, with their four children
Left to right: on Kuqui's lap, Sara; on Martin's lap, Mirella; Lieta, Malena and
Natasha, 2002

Lieta with her brothers and sisters: left to right standing: Maria Angelica, Neldi
Mercedes and Cecilia. Sitting - left to right: Mele, Lieta, Kuqui, 2002

Neldi, Lieta and
Taisaku,
Argentina 2002

Lieta with
Silvina,
September
2002

Lieta greets Chiara,
October 2002

Chapter 15

Radiant Light

1998 was a year of great light and joy. On the 16th January, Lieta and Bruno sat in the small front lounge in Curryhills House, and signed the deeds for the new Mariapolis Centre. It seemed a miracle. It had all happened so fast - finding the property and finding the money to buy it. The movement had been saving for a while to purchase a centre, but nothing prepared Lieta for the amazing out-pouring of providence when the deal finally became a reality. Every day money arrived from the focolare community all over Ireland - from small sums, to very large.

Rejoicing in this miracle she wrote: "We feel engulfed by a wave of the Holy Spirit. Every day we have to follow that voice well and we are at peace because everything goes ahead in a truly breathtaking adventure."

Nine days after the close of the sale, three focolarine moved to Curryhills House - Maria Smoelz from Germany, Emma Kim from Korea and Catherine Burke from Ireland - welcomed by a huge bunch of flowers from the Travers family, its previous owners. Lieta confided that things were going so well that she was afraid that she would become attached to the beautiful things of the earth, but then she reminded herself that material things would pass and what counted was her love for Jesus, to live her life for Him, and with the others to have His presence among them. "The more you put yourself to one side, the better everything goes and there is Jesus among us with His joy and love," she wrote to a friend.

It was a time of full joy. "In the past during some moments of the life of focolare, I experienced such a love for Jesus, that it made me sing," she wrote. "On other occasions, which were a little rarer, I remember feeling that I was ready, if God were to call me, to go to Him and I told him so. And now that time has come back."

Lieta lived in the focolare centre in Dublin, but day by day she monitored the developments at the new Mariapolis Centre, which Chiara had named 'Radiosa' or 'Radiant Light'. Maria, Emma and Catherine were living in a few rooms upstairs in the old part of the Georgian building. It was a tough time for them - a lot of cleaning and sorting out to be done and the house was very cold. The only heating was an old solid fuel system. Hundreds of wood pallets were stacked near the turkey barn, and in order to have hot water or heating, the women had to get the fire going with the pallets early each morning, and feed it every few hours. Maria was working in Naas, Catherine in Dublin.

Emma was alone during the day. She had never lived in the country before. Lieta tried to get down to her as often as possible, helping her to see the positive in the strange experiences she was going through - like finding a panicked bird in one of the rooms, or plucking a dead mouse from under the floorboards with chop sticks.

The whole focolare community rejoiced over the purchase of Curryhills house, and it immediately became a focal point, with people coming each weekend to see it and to help.

On a spring weekend, Bruno worked to get a huge iron cooker out of the kitchen, eventually taking a hammer to it. At the entrance gate, Donal O'Byrne (who later moved to Prosperous), worked with Maria, power hosing the pillars. Eoin Barry and John Bevan from Cork pulled weeds and cut hedges in the garden. Nearby, Lieta painted a fence.

She was aware that this was a moment of special light for the Focolare in Ireland. She and Bruno went to tell the local bishop, Laurence Ryan, that they were thinking of having their headquarters in his diocese. His welcome was warm and whole-hearted, sentiments repeated by the other bishops too. Cardinal Cahal Daly told Lieta and Bruno that it was a moment of God for Ireland.

"We saw providence come from every corner of Ireland," recalls Bruno. "You could feel the hand of

God in every detail - from the gas passing the gate of the Mariapolis centre, and their agreeing to link us up to the mains free of charge. The water came, including a pipe from the back and the sewage system. At times I felt Mary was walking in the little town. The tarmac of the road (from the gate to the car park) was a free gift from the County Council. Mary was walking up the avenue and she needed a good road," remarked Bruno.

The women's focolare centre in Templeogue was sold and in a short time more than 80 per cent of the purchase price was raised. When Chiara originally saw the plans of the centre and its grounds, she had exclaimed "But this is a 'little town' of witness". And this was ultimately the desire of the whole Focolare family in Ireland - for the centre to be not just a place where people would gather at weekends, with a small group of focolarini living there, but a little town bringing together men, women, families, single people, religious and children.

Lieta and Bruno set out to make this happen. Firstly, they agreed to move the two zone centres from Dublin to Prosperous. The first hurdle was to get planning permission. The plans were drawn and submitted and everyone started to pray. The O'Brien family in Kilkenny had expressed an interest in moving to Prosperous. Lieta encouraged them wholeheartedly. She believed in people and this gave them confidence. Declan O'Brien had just got a new job and he realised that it would be possible to commute to it from Prosperous. "Go for it!" said Lieta, but she advised them that all of their five children had to be happy about the move. At the time the children ranged in age from nineteen to five.

One night the O'Brien family gathered for a family conference. Back in Dublin Lieta and Bruno waited anxiously to hear the outcome. In the end all of the children were happy except one of the older boys who had left school and was strongly attached to Kilkenny. But he said to go ahead - he would not be there and it was their life. Afterwards Lieta remarked that his was the most "profound choice" because he was going against his own desires.

The O'Brien family managed to sell their house in Kilkenny in record time, and bought a house in the village of Prosperous from plans. Their daughter Kate, who was starting her senior cycle at school, moved in to Curryhills House in September, followed a month later by her Mum and Dad and two sisters. They set up temporary home in a downstairs apartment of Curryhills House.

It was a new experience to have a family living at Radiosa. Lieta was anxious that their family life and autonomy be respected. As people gathered for a meeting one weekend, Lieta made an announcement - if was a rest weekend, no-one was to call on the O'Briens. "They need their break!"

Christmas was a merry occasion. Lieta and all the

focolarine from Dublin celebrated together at the Mariapolis Centre. On St Stephen's Day the O'Briens joined them for dinner. Afterwards they sat around the Christmas tree and sang songs. "It was a real family moment," recalls Declan.

In March 1999 Lieta and Bruno got the great news that they had planning permission and could start building the women's zone centre at the back of the Mariapolis Radiosa. The news came on the 25th March, feast of the Annunciation, almost like a gift from Mary to the Focolare Movement which has the official name, Work of Mary. Lieta and Bruno saw the hand of God in this circumstance too. There was also planning permission for the men's zone centre, and a house for priests.

Meanwhile in Dublin, Lieta was immersing herself in a new reality which was coming to life world-wide within the movement - the promotion of unity between lay Catholic movements. In 1998, they had all come together for the first time in Rome with Pope John Paul II. Now was the moment for groups to meet at a national level. In Ireland the gathering was planned for 23rd May 1999 in University College Dublin. Lieta and Bruno, together with the leaders of other movements like Charismatic Renewal, Communion and Liberation and the St Egidio Community, were in the thick of the preparations. In the end over 1,000 people took part in the historic gathering.

At the end of the summer, Lieta moved to the Mariapolis Radiosa, and Bruno moved to a house in the village of Prosperous and prepared for his ordination to the priesthood. The O'Brien's home was ready and they settled down to live in the village. Construction began on the women's focolare centre and at the back of the centre, a small cottage for visitors was being renovated.

It was very busy and tiring with all the building work going on. One day Lieta was so tired that she felt she had not the energy to love anyone. She felt a sinner. During Mass she thought of Jesus on the cross crying out 'Why'. She chose to love him, as the One who felt like a sinner. "I tried to rejoice because He has already paid," she wrote. "Once I made that jump into Him, I re-entered the light, the Gospel and I thanked God for having this experience, for having Jesus forsaken the 'super love' who transforms everything into love."

She stayed on her guard to be always empathising with those around her, and not to let all the practical work take over her life. One day there was a retreat for focolarine at Radiosa. At the end Lieta invited anyone who wanted a chat to come and see her in a sitting room upstairs. While the others went off for a walk and a coffee, Paula came in. Lieta looked at her and saw she was upset. Paula sat down on a low spongy brown chair. She was passing through a difficult moment, but did not know how to describe it. She said things were tough and began to cry. Lieta got up, walked across to her, and knelt beside the chair and held her. "After ten or fifteen minutes, I'd stopped crying and we were there in silence. She continued to embrace me," recalls Paula. "At the end I said 'I think I needed that.' I was resolved."

She goes on: "Lieta loved each person with that measure - in God. It is a strong argument for celibacy - the fact that you can reach a relationship that is so human and so deep, so there is no need for one particular person."

Towards the end of 1999 the cottage at Radiosa was almost complete. Who would live there? Lieta cast her eye around the people she knew and her look came to rest on Anna, a Volunteer from Dublin, who was working in Newbridge. One day Anna was at the centre and Lieta invited her to come and see the newly completed cottage. She showed her around, and then gently asked: "Would you like to come and live here?" Anna was delighted. Practically speaking it made a lot of sense, cutting her daily commute by two thirds. She said yes, and two months later she was ensconced in the cottage, where she lived for three years. The Mariapolis Radiosa had another resident.

In February 2000 a family of four moved to Prosperous, this time from Dublin. Lieta was in the house waiting to help as the removal truck pulled up outside their new house and she stationed herself in the kitchen, unpacking boxes of delph. "As we worked together, she gave me a great lesson in harmony," recalls Susan, "throwing out chipped cups, saucers and bowls. Each time she would turn to me with a twinkle in her eye and say 'Will I throw this out?' One mouldy wooden fruit bowl had been in my family for decades. 'Will I throw it out?' 'Yes,' I answered, with a little twinge. A few days later a friend gave me a present of a beautiful new wooden fruit bowl which her husband had made by hand. God always gives us back what we lose for him!"

Six months later Lieta was welcoming another family, this time from Cork. Bill and Máire O'Brien and their three children moved to live in Prosperous. By the end of 2000, the Mariapolis Radiosa, so much rooted in her heart, had over 20 inhabitants - men and women focolarini, families, single people and children.

She dreamt of Chiara coming to visit the newest 'little town' of the movement. On a cold winter's night in November, over a meal, she confided this deep held desire to the local parish priest, Fr Jackie Connell, who was having dinner with them. "I'll light a candle in my house when I get home and I'll leave it lit until Chiara comes," he promised Lieta.

Chapter 16

Dusk

2001. Lieta used to say that she had the stomach of a goat, and could eat anything. But this was to change. She began to have stomach problems and feel tired. Even a holiday in the sun did not make her feel better. The holiday was beautiful, but she was getting tired quickly. Her stomach felt sick. On her return she went to see the doctor and got blood tests. Maybe it is my stage in life, she thought, realising she was approaching fifty. As she awaited the results, she thought that this was a new face of her spouse, Jesus forsaken. "How beautiful - You Lord are my only good," she wrote, underlining the word 'only'.

More tests in March and April... Lieta tried to rest more, to pace herself. The Focolare Day Meeting had been cancelled because of the 'Foot and Mouth' scare so it was a quieter period. Often however she persevered, ignoring nausea, back pain or her lack of energy. One weekend she had a demanding meeting, and afterwards a chat with someone. Later she wrote in her diary: "I wasn't very well."

Lieta shared her concerns about her health with Gis, her mentor at the centre of the movement. Gis told her not to hesitate to stop if she needed to rest. "You'll see, doing the will of God, you will attract many graces to Ireland and Mary will bring everything ahead herself."

The results of Lieta's tests came through in May. She was alright. According to the scan, her stomach was normal, but she might have had fibroids. Everyone rejoiced and Lieta breathed a sigh of relief. But she wondered why she still felt unwell ...

In June she celebrated her 50th birthday. She wanted it to be a simple celebration and invited twenty or so friends to share a meal with her at an unpretentious restaurant. Beside her sat an old friend, a lady Lieta had looked after for many years. She had a psychiatric illness and wavered between jovial acceptance of her customary ill health, and extreme depressive delusions coupled with severe physical hardship. For over twenty five years, Lieta had been a sister to her. That night, although it was Lieta's party, the focus was on her good friend Clare.

The annual summer gathering that year took place in Prosperous. Lieta looked radiant, the picture of good health, but she was not feeling well. Each day she quietly withdrew and went to bed for a while when she had not the strength to stay with people. And in her own words, "The Mariapolis went better than ever!"

Two bishops, the bishop of Kildare, Laurence Ryan and an auxiliary bishop of Dublin, Ray Field, spent time at the Mariapolis. In addition, the Ambassador of Slovakia was a special guest. "It has been a real triumph of Jesus in our midst among the 450 participants," Lieta wrote.

In the months ahead she was back and forth to three different hospitals for thyroid, intestinal and gynaecological tests. As she returned from another holiday, still not feeling well, a new understanding was blossoming in her: "Love and not activism has to grow," she wrote.

With Bruno, her co-responsible for the movement, Lieta tried to live "the new unity". This phrase, coined by Chiara at the time, was a unity beyond all differences. Looking at Lieta and Bruno, people were touched to see such a strong bond between them - how they communicated each day, letting go of ideas, taking up others. Following their example, the whole movement had become more one, with more interaction and sharing between men and women and between different branches.

"This unity with Lieta was like a game. It was to live with great simplicity," said Bruno. "She was a sister for me and a mother and a daughter in a way. We were living so much in unity that where I went, she went, whether I went to Cork, or she went to Belfast, everything belonged to Jesus in our midst - nothing to me, nothing to her, so everything had to be given back to Jesus in the midst."

That autumn, Chiara asked for an even deeper

supernatural bond between the delegates, where each person (starting with the delegates), would live not just for their own reality or responsibility, but for the reality of the other. At the meeting with the zone of Ireland, and some other western European regions, there was a great togetherness, and the focolare founder felt free to really speak her mind. Listening to her, Lieta felt as if she was being told off. It was a suffering. For a moment she was upset, but then chose Jesus on the cross once again, as her only good.

But her dismay quickly turned to joy when the news came through that Chiara was thinking of coming to Ireland. Three girls came to live at the cottage in the Mariapolis Radiosa, bringing the presence of young people to Ireland's 'little town'. For Lieta it was another essential element. Radiosa was ready to welcome Chiara. Her heart was full of joy as she contemplated the new developments, but day by day physically she felt less well. Calling it a 'bug,' she took days of rest and did more tests. Perhaps this trial was the price to pay to merit at first hand the gift of having Chiara in Ireland.

Early in December 2001 Lieta went on holidays to Tenerife with her friend Mari who immediately noticed how her health had disimproved. Lieta could only swim for a few minutes and often felt unwell. She was eating only small amounts of food. One evening Mari walked the rather long distance to the church in Los Cristianos. Lieta stayed at home. On the way back, walking towards the flat, Mari began to see flashes around her and feared she was getting a detached retina. When Lieta answered the door to her, she immediately realised that Mari was frightened. "I remember she stayed with me like a mother. The next day she had to leave in the afternoon but she accompanied me to the hospital and stayed there for hours, until I got to know that my retina was not detached as we all feared, but it was a much more minor ailment," recalls Mari.

In January 2002, Lieta accompanied a group of married focolarine to Rome. It was a very hard meeting for her. She was in continuous pain, agitated, irritated. She could not get comfortable. Everything annoyed her. She found it difficult to eat because nothing was sitting well in her stomach, but she made herself eat. With supreme effort she masked her discomfort, chatting to those around her and trying to be her usual happy self.

During the meeting, she had a chance to greet Chiara in the corridor. "Ireland is waiting for you, Chiara," she told her, and hope grew.

That same month, she was due to visit her family in Argentina for a few weeks. She was very sick, but did not want to postpone the journey. A new Brazilian focolarina arrived in Ireland. Jucemara was 23 and this was her first time to be part of a focolare community.

Before she left, Lieta called Jucemara into the living room. "I'm sorry for leaving you now but it's only for three weeks. Juanita will look after you. Remember to live making a lot of pacts with Jesus" she told her with great love. "She understood I liked elderly people. Before she left, she told me 'It would be nice if you could have the same love for young people as you have for the elderly when you move to Dublin'," Jucemara recalls.

Paula Dowd was to bring her to the airport. Paula was a nurse and Lieta knew she was looking at her with a look that told her that she wanted to bring her to hospital or at least put her to bed. She avoided her look.

"I remember she shunned me," Paula recalls. "She knew she had to get on that plane. I was thinking 'You are so sick. I should go to the hospital. I can't bring you. I shouldn't bring you.' She was looking at me with a look that said 'Who's boss here. I've had enough. Stay in your place'."

So with a heavy heart, Paula brought her to the airport and Lieta departed for her homeland. It would be a long time before she was back on Irish soil again.

Chapter 17

Return to Argentina

Lieta got back to Argentina. She was weary and in pain when she arrived. At the airport, Neldi and other family members gave her a rapturous welcome. But they immediately saw that Lieta was not well. She had lost weight and seemed a little agitated. As if realising that she would not have strength for very long, she wanted to immediately visit her family, to distribute gifts and money. Neldi, her sister, urged her to rest after the long journey. All that could wait.

"It was as if she was in a hurry to do everything," Neldi recalls. "Before, when I used to come to meetings in Rome, or when we saw each other in Argentina, I would see a Lieta who was always joyful, always in a disposition of love, open and sympathetic. There I saw Lieta in fear, in weakness, needing to be embraced and loved with a natural, sisterly love."

Neldi and the family immediately arranged for Lieta to take a weeklong holiday by the sea, but this did no good. Every second day Lieta was in touch with Neldi asking to see a doctor and to have further tests done. By now she could not eat at all: everything was coming back up. She knew she was in trouble. Through Dr Beatric Lauren, a focolarina specialising in gastroenterology, Lieta was able to have an early appointment with a specialist, a doctor of Irish origin. Immediately he admitted her to the hospital and became like a father figure, sitting on the bed and explaining procedures to her.

Lieta was in fear. On the phone she described to Neldi what the specialist had told her - her stomach was like a pot with no hole. Surgery was imperative. It was scheduled for 8th February 2002. Beforehand they took a biopsy. In her life as a focolarina, Lieta had accompanied many people to the door of Paradise, but she herself had a deep rooted fear of death. In a letter in 1989 she wrote "I've always been a little frightened of death.....". Now this fear was to return as she faced surgery.

The biopsy showed a malignant tumour but Lieta was unaware of this. When Neldi found out she was devastated. She sensed Lieta did not want to have confirmation of bad news before her operation. As she went to visit her the night before, she wondered how on earth she would manage to keep the news to herself. Just one look at her grief stricken face and Lieta would know all.

But that night providence intervened to keep the news of the tumour a secret. Lia, the co-director of the Focolare in Argentina and another good friend of Lieta's were visiting her just before Neldi was due and they cheered her up. When Neldi and

Beatric went in, Lieta was happy. "She didn't want to know what she knew already," said Neldi. She and Beatric said nothing about the biopsy results. "We thought, 'Here God himself has taken things in hand and He knows.' And Lieta was preparing for the operation the next day, like that."

The operation turned out to be much more serious than anticipated. The tumour was very advanced. Awaking after the operation, Lieta smiled gently at Neldi. "It went well, didn't it?" she asked. "Yes," replied Neldi "Very well. Now you just rest."

Lieta spent the whole of the day after her operation in silence. Her friend Elda, another doctor, had advised her not to speak to avoid vomiting. Lieta followed her advice to the letter, so much so that nurses feared the operation had left her mute.

She was in a public hospital ward with five other patients. Lieta praised the nurses for their dedication and love. Conditions were basic but the atmosphere was one of calm and joy, which touched the other patients too. At a certain point one day, the nurses, patients and Neldi were joking, and they all broke into a childhood song. Lieta was laughing in the relaxed atmosphere. "Truly you learn a lot being close to a sick person and the Gospel helps us strike the right note, where you can play tricks, joke, and laugh without losing the solemnity of the present moment," Neldi wrote to Juanita.

Lieta was very weak. She knew something was

wrong, but did not ask about it. She was conserving her strength. She realised that facing additional anxiety would just sap her strength. Her focus was on recuperating. Two nights after the operation, Neldi arrived with a beautiful bouquet of musket roses from Bruno and a plant from Lia. They were magnificent flowers. Lieta suggested giving them away to the patient in the opposite bed. The lady was thrilled to see her little table adorned with the cheery flowers. After a while Lieta whispered to Neldi "I'm enjoying those flowers more now because before they were behind me and I couldn't see them." Having given away the flowers they became a gift for her.

But within days, a huge trial began for Lieta. She was agitated and afraid. She missed her Irish family desperately. She worried about the uncertainty of the future. She felt she had not done God's will during the time she led the movement in Ireland. For three days she was in spiritual darkness.

A letter arrived from Chiara. "With you I live your meeting with the Spouse [Jesus forsaken] who has made Himself present in this illness, certainly out of His plan of love," wrote the Focolare founder, and she urged Lieta to abandon herself trustingly to God's will, by doing the necessary treatments well. The letter allayed some of Lieta's fear. That night she was a little more serene and in Neldi's words "the next day I had the impression that a patch of blue was opening in the sky". When she left she had the impression "the Madonna was close to her".

In Ireland the news of the gravity of Lieta's illness spread like wildfire and there was a spontaneous outpouring of love towards her - emails, gifts, money and prayers for her complete recovery.

The love coming back from the land she loved so well was like a supernatural drip for her soul. Weak though she was, she tried to follow every person, every activity. She rejoiced to hear that forty priests had been to a seminar at the Mariapolis Centre. The bishop of Kildare, Dr Laurence Ryan, had dropped in on the gathering too, and at the end of the day, he had thanked the movement for the good it was doing in his diocese and in the country.

She wanted to hear the voices of the focolarine from her focolare in Kildare. The hospital was enormous and it was difficult to get access to a public phone. So every so often she escaped in her pyjamas to a shop down the road, where she could ring Ireland. In the early days of Lieta's recuperation, Neldi was her mainstay, also because her other sisters were away. Neldi realised that she needed to take care of her own health and one day decided to visit a friend of hers, Taisaku. He was a Japanese Buddhist and an expert in Chinese medicine and massage. The year before he had been to the Mariapolis where Neldi had shared her story, telling of her sister Lieta, and how, as children, they used to help each other to live the Gospel at home. Taisaku was impressed by this story.

When Neldi told Taisaku about Lieta in hospital, he immediately wanted to come to see her, to help. Neldi agreed, but told him that she would have to talk to Lieta first to see if it was alright with her. In bed in hospital, Lieta heard for the first time about Taisaku and his offer to give her a massage. She did not like the sound of it at all. "He can't touch me! I don't like those strange things!" she told Neldi. "He just wants to meet you," Neldi said. In the end Lieta agreed.

When Taisaku came in, Neldi immediately had a new sensation - through Lieta she was witnessing first hand unity between cultures, religions and brothers - universal brotherhood.

They talked for a while. Lieta asked him to help her "because I have to go home. I have to go back to Ireland". After talking for a while, Taisaku offered some alternative therapy to Lieta, not touching her at all, but transmitting a great calm to her. Afterwards she slept deeply for the first time.

This was the beginning of a luminous relationship between the Japanese Buddhist and Lieta. "He was like an angel, a person God put there to help her to find that balance and to take away the fear that was so strong, because every change was dramatic for her," Neldi recalls. Taisaku became a regular visitor to Lieta even after she left hospital. Over time she learned to lose the desire to return to Ireland and realised she had to be looked after in Argentina.

Meanwhile at her bedside in the hospital, each day the women from the focolare centre in Buenos Aires spent long periods with her. This became a great gift for each one, as Lieta willingly shared her experiences of life in focolare with them, humbly admitting the many mistakes she had made along the way so they would not repeat them. They were precious lessons.

After three weeks, Lieta heard she could leave hospital and recuperate at home. In joy she wrote to Chiara: "I feel that EVERYTHING has been HIS GRACE and I want to correspond with all my heart, repeating to him now: You, with Mary Desolate, are my only good."

Chapter 18

Running

On the 21st February 2002, Lieta moved back into the zone centre focolare of Buenos Aires to recuperate from her surgery. Living with her were her close friend and confidante, Ines, her sister Neldi and other focolarine. The operation had left her weak and in pain. Her last day in hospital was hard. There were problems with the drip and her wound was not closing properly. Grumbling and in pain, everything annoyed her. But when she finally reached the focolare centre, she was full of joy and relief.

Her presence brought a new atmosphere and harmony. For the next weeks Lieta was the hub of the zone centre. She tried hard to eat and put on weight as with the blockage in her stomach she had not eaten for 25 days.

There was a small chapel in the house and Lieta became a regular visitor to Jesus in the Eucharist. She grew to depend on His constant support and urged Juanita back in Ireland to complete the chapel in the zone centre there so that they too could have His presence at home. She was delighted when the chapel in her home in Kildare was officially opened on 16th March 2002.

For the first time in months, Lieta was able to take part in the weekly meeting of the focolare. It was a great gift. She felt she was living between two fires - the fire of the presence of Jesus within her and his presence in the midst of the focolare.

A Salesian priest came to visit and had a conversation with Lieta. Afterwards he told Neldi: "I saw a soul identified with Jesus forsaken, completely in the darkness and completely in the light."

For Neldi it was a joy to have her sister home, but a strain too. She felt they were playing hide and seek, each pretending to the other that things were better than they were - Lieta not letting on how ill she felt, Neldi not revealing how much she suffered to see her sister so ground down. Lieta still did not know the result of her operation. She did not know that a large malignant tumour had been removed. She did not know the prognosis. Time passed and no one had the courage to break the silence. Then one weekend Lieta's sister Kuqui came to look after her. Lieta was in bed, not strong enough to get up. At the time she was not eating and was in pain. Kuqui, married to a doctor, was a straight talking person.

At a certain moment she and Lieta were alone. "I don't know if I have something 'bad' or if I'm getting better," Lieta said to her. "Yes, you have cancer," Kuqui told her bluntly. The mask was off. When Neldi came home later that day, Lieta's look told her she knew everything. "From that day forward we learnt to live with the present moment, not with the illness - to play fully with life," recounts Neldi.

Shortly after Lieta had her first appointment with an oncologist. Even the word "oncologist" terrified her. She was still living at the zone centre, but it was rapidly becoming clear that this was not the right place for her to be. Her friends found a special apartment for her, with Elda a doctor, Silvina, Norma who had MS and Sarucha, who would help look after the others.

When the subject was broached, Lieta reacted negatively - she did not want to move. "I prefer to be here in this focolare," she answered. She did not want to be without Neldi, without the chapel, without her confidante Ines.

Nonetheless she took the step and by mid March was in her new home which was on the 8th floor of a skyscraper. It was bright and airy, but for Lieta its location in the heart of the city heightened her trial. She had come from the green fields of Kildare, countryside and quiet, and suddenly she found herself very ill and living in a skyscraper in a huge, noisy, crowded city. It all served to make the trial even bigger and the desire to escape stronger - to return, to return to Ireland.

Her new focolare was very different to the zone centre focolare. Here there was no emphasis on activities or the movement, just on living with the presence of Jesus in the midst. It was a competition of love. There were jokes and laughter. Lieta stored up the jokes to bring back to Ireland.

She shared a bedroom with Silvina who became her personal assistant and accompanied her each time to the chemo sessions. Silvina had been through cancer and chemotherapy herself so she knew what Lieta was going through. In the beginning she felt a certain barrier between them - the barrier of human respect. Lieta was older and wiser, but soon Lieta dissolved this barrier and the two became inseparable.

Her friends placed great emphasis on her food - searching for anything she might enjoy eating. Sarucha, a great cook, invented dishes to whet Lieta's appetite. Everything was cooked fresh, nothing reheated. Then they used to sit for hours around the table, chatting, telling jokes, trying to get Lieta to eat a little more. She still had the appetite of a bird. Still it was a place of love. One person described that focolare centre as a 'magnet'.

On 18th March 2002, Lieta travelled to the public hospital for her first chemo session. Fifteen people sat in the room with one nurse giving injections to each person in turn. She was fast because she had to be. She came to Lieta whose veins collapsed and the nurse could not get the needle in, making the pain much worse. Lieta's fear increased. It was a horrible day.

On the way home she sat in silence and stayed that way for hours. Silvina, who had herself just finished treatment for cancer knew what Lieta was feeling. It had been the same for her when she was ill. "I used to think: 'You've done everything badly so he's taking everything away'," Silvina recalls. She thought Lieta was beginning to go through something similar. On the outside she was smiling though other times she was more rigid. It was as if she was saying to herself, "God is asking this of me, so I have to do it."

But with time, this changed. Lieta was like someone who entered into what God asked of her. Even so, when she got home she told Neldi "I don't want to do it again, I'd prefer to die." But then she put herself into the reality of love, writing a letter to her old friend Bishop O'Mahony in Ireland. "This is the secret of my life now," she wrote, "living the present moment well and experiencing the help of actual grace. For example, when I have to sleep, I say to myself: I have to do this to perfection and I really sleep well!"

That day she also wrote to the whole Irish community for the Day Meeting which took place on 24th March 2002. This was the single biggest gathering in the Focolare calendar for the year. "I'm having treatment which will last for a few months. So in this present moment, through these circumstances, God has asked me to let go of Ireland."

The 2002 Day meeting was a special moment in the history of the Focolare in Ireland. After twenty six years in the country, Bruno was leaving for Australia. The gathering that day was his official farewell party. It was a day marked with joy and great gratitude for his enormous contribution to the lives of the people of the Focolare, and tinged with sadness that he was leaving. Added to this was the poignancy that Lieta, the woman who had shared so much and lived through so much with him, was not there to witness the sketches, songs and dances dedicated to him, including a country and western parody, "You picked a fine time to leave us, Bruno".

Lieta was living that day with them. With all her heart she wanted to be there, but she let this desire go, and concentrated instead on pouring her love into her letter. "Today is the occasion to say good-bye to Bruno and as you can imagine I feel a great gratitude in my heart for these many years of life during which, with many of you, despite our own limits, we built the reality of the Movement spiritually and now concretely through the little town Radiosa, providing a permanent place for Jesus in the midst in our country, a kind of 'cradle' where we can give witness to Him and go forward towards 'that all may be one'."

Easter was coming. A chocolate Easter rabbit arrived from Ireland, and immediately Lieta thought of sending it to the young people at Mariapolis O'Higgins in Argentina. Each day she found a way to love the people she was with. "She was like a luminous lighthouse, a real gift, because notwithstanding the trial which was very strong- the physical trial and the trial inside her-no one escaped her love," says Neldi.

In a letter to Chiara around Easter Lieta wrote: "On waking this morning I put myself immediately in Jesus forsaken, to live each moment with Him. You are here with me, and I am with you. I offer every- thing...... and I'm running."

Chapter 19

Chemo and Coffee

Back in Ireland, Lieta's suffering was bearing huge fruit. The Irish President, Mary McAleese, who had come in contact with people of the movement, said she would be happy to meet its founder if she visited Ireland, and dates were discussed. Suddenly the chance that Chiara might visit Ireland in 2003 became a real possibility.

On 14th April 2002, Chiara greeted a group of Irish young people at a meeting in Rome for those considering a vocation to the focolare, and she told them that "maybe I will come to Ireland next year when I go to Britain". The visit to the UK was scheduled for May 2003. The Focolare community was overjoyed and immediately went into overdrive to get ready for the visit which they saw as a direct fruit of Lieta's suffering.

From Argentina, Lieta dispensed practical advice to prepare for Chiara's visit - "Paint the flagpoles. Paint the door to the Mariapolis Centre red. Put a handrail on the steps," she instructed. "We did everything she suggested," recalls Juanita.

Meanwhile her painful monthly chemo sessions

continued. When Silvina was undergoing her own chemo, she used to go for coffee afterwards. "I used to tell myself: 'God only asked that one thing of me' [the chemo session]." She invited Lieta to go for coffee afterwards, as she had done, but Lieta would not consider it. She wanted to get home to see if there was news from Ireland, to keep up with the activities of the movement. Often she was disappointed to find that the mail just consisted of greetings and people wishing her well.

In May, coming up to halfway through her chemo, Lieta finally had direct contact with her Irish family, when Paula arrived for a three week stay. She found a very different Lieta. When she arrived, the other women greeted Paula warmly, but there was no sign of Lieta. She asked "Where's Lieta?" and then spotted her skirting around the edges, holding back.

"I understood that she was living in such darkness that she couldn't believe I had come. There was the trial of the cancer and fighting it, but by separating her from Ireland, God had taken everything. So [to her] it seemed it couldn't be true that someone had arrived from Ireland."

Paula spotted Lieta out of the corner of her eye. "Something told me not to run to her. When I saw her, I saw this skeleton of six and a half stone." She was shocked at her physical appearance and realised Lieta was not ready to say hello. "Her character had changed. I felt I was meeting another Lieta."

Paula was overflowing with love for her. But this was not the moment to show it. She had to be empty, respectful of where Lieta was at. "I had to be emptiness in being there immediately for her. Not to be as I had thought - abounding love for her from everyone in Ireland."

"She looked at me with a look that said 'Look at how different I am.' I just held her. She said 'Do you recognise me?'" Soon after, the other women departed, and Paula was left alone with Lieta. "What will we do now?" she asked. "I'd like to wash my hair," Lieta replied. As she washed Lieta's hair, clumps fell into the sink. Lieta reached for a tissue. "Look what you have come for. You have come to love this Jesus forsaken," she said as she cleared the hair on the edges of the sink with a tissue.

Lieta and Paula spoke very little for the first few days, but she immediately allowed Paula to be part of her, "her arms, her legs, her shadow". She was so thin that she had marks on her arms and heels after lying down, so Paula would massage her muscles before she got up. Meanwhile Lieta continued to play the game of living only the present moment. She wrote to Chiara "I feel in a privileged position because thanks to the sickness and treatments, I am obliged to 'savour' the present moment." Paula and those around joined in the game.

She wanted to bring Paula to see the Focolare's little town in Argentina, O'Higgins. There was a hiatus period between chemo sessions where she had a little more strength. This would be the time to go for it, and take the long journey to O'Higgins. Lieta made the suggestion and they went along with her desire. On the way they would call in to the Marian shrine of Lujan.

There was a terrible storm as they were leaving. Lieta was weak and ill getting into the car. But she was determined to go. By now she knew that her condition was very serious and was praying for a cure. At the Marian shrine she told the others: "Foco[19] needs miracles to become a saint." Theirs would be a miracle of mutual love, she thought, his intercession providing her recovery, her miracle bringing him a step closer to sanctity.

The storm passed and they travelled across the rich pampas lands of central Argentina, reminiscent of the Curragh of Kildare. The music of a well known Argentinean female vocalist blared through the radio as they travelled. They were happy. At one point they stopped and took a photo of the beautiful horizon.

The weekend at O'Higgins was like a balm for Lieta's soul as she became immersed once again in the life of the movement, hearing updates and news, meeting the other focolarini, seeing her sister Kuqui and her family. She began to pick up again.

---

[19] Foco, or Igino Giordani, was a member of the Italian Parliament and the first married focolarino. He is seen as a co-founder of the Focolare Movement. He died in 1980. His cause of canonization is presently underway.

On 18th May 2002, she, Neldi and Kuqui visited their Dad's grave together.

But on her return from O'Higgins she faced a difficult week. On Tuesday she went for a CAT scan. She was to get the results two days later, but was too ill to go. That night her temperature spiked. Lieta was rushed to the hospital in the middle of the night. Paula and Tecla stayed behind, saying the rosary as they waited for news. Tests were carried out. It turned out the dye used in the scan had caused an infection, but her white cells were fighting it and she was going to be ok. In the middle of the night they returned home. Everyone was waiting for them, and they celebrated having Lieta home, and knowing that she was ok. "I remember from then it was like the beginning of the recovery," recalls Paula. "She started to get well. That night the change seemed for the worst, but it was for the best."

Lieta was due to return to the hospital for the results of the scan but could not face it, so Neldi and Silvina went in her place. They updated the specialist on her progress. He confessed that he had not had the courage to tell Lieta exactly what she had, which was a cancer of the blood affecting the white cells. The tumour in Lieta's stomach was a secondary. She was responding to the treatment but she was not in the clear, and he wanted her to have another three sessions of chemotherapy. Overall though, the news was good.

A few days later Lieta herself met the oncologist. By then she had lost her fear and had established such a close relationship with the specialist that he asked her about her life. She opened her soul to him. "Do you know that from the time I was a child I found this ideal of God. I made this choice in freedom but with this illness I feel he has come to take for Himself that first place I had given him, that with the years had been filled with many other things." The doctor was moved by her words and decided he would find out more about the Focolare. Later he visited the Mariapolis Lia.

In the end, he proposed a second round of chemo. A depressing thought. Inside Lieta a niggling question was going around her mind. Could she dare ask the doctor? She would. "What about Rome, do you think I can go there in the autumn?" He paused for a moment. "You probably can," he said. "Why not?" Lieta's face became luminous. She was immensely happy. Immediately they went to celebrate with ice cream.

As Paula departed for Ireland, it seemed Lieta had turned a corner. One day she even managed a ten minute walk and was feeling stronger. On 30th May 2002, she wrote to Chiara saying that now that she felt better, she had to be careful not to draw away from the "divine logic" of suffering love that she lived before: "I don't want to lose it." She promised to count the number of times she loved Jesus in suffering, so as to keep her love for him 'fresh'.

Paula returned to Ireland where the focolare community was anxiously awaiting news. In Lieta's absence they too had changed. Through her illness, it seemed the movement had become even more of a family.

Meanwhile Lieta began her second round of chemo, this time at a private clinic. By now she had established such a strong rapport with the nurses and her fellow patients at the first hospital, that she was reluctant to change. "Here I feel that I'm the same as everyone, I am like all the people," she told Silvina, happy to identify with people who had no money or other possibilities.

During the second round of chemo, her state of soul changed. She entered the relationship with God and was happy to do what He wanted. So after the fourth chemo session she said to Silvina, "Let's go for a coffee." This became a pattern - after chemo came coffee and a walk. On the fifth round Lieta had not even the strength to go for a walk, but she still said: "Let's go." "We went into the park, we walked, we stopped. She entered that place of not wanting to do her own will," recalls Silvina.

As time passed, Silvina became like an extension of Lieta. They would go to the chemo sessions together. On the way, Silvina would navigate and Lieta drive as they said the rosary. Returning they reversed the process. They shared a bedroom at night. It was a dynamic situation with its ups and downs.

One morning Lieta came back to the room to discover that Silvina had made her bed. It annoyed her as she felt she could have managed it herself. Silvina was in bed, and Lieta turned around and went out to the kitchen. "Afterwards she came in to go to bed," Silvina recounts. "'Silvina let's start again,' she said to me. We didn't let any moment pass without love, even if there were those moments of tension, Lieta was always first to start again."

Another day, she woke very early in the morning after a bad night where she had woken several times. "Silvina, did you feel fear in front of death?" she asked her friend. Silvina frankly told her what she had felt one day. They spoke for almost an hour. Lieta confided her fear of going before God with things half done. "I've done everything badly, but during this time, I have learnt to love God" she told her. She had fallen in love with Jesus forsaken and only now was she really getting to know him.

On other occasions she cried during the night, feeling a failure, wanting to start over. But gradually she abandoned herself to God. At times she wanted to stay with people and then afterwards was not well. Little by little she understood that this was neither good for her or other people. She began to actively listen to what God was telling her and then had the freedom to say: "Come tomorrow. I may be in bed. If I want to, I'll get up." Her state of soul was transformed into love, and how she felt, whether well or badly, did not matter. Lieta understood that life was not a 'doing' but a 'being' - being love in front of the other, being for the other in each present moment.

In July she wrote to Paola Monetta, a focolarina back in Ireland. "'Not being' is my experience. It is what is best for others. When we suffer, it seems to me that others are well. I wonder why that should be? When I am better and I want 'to do' many things, I come up against the limits of the other person. Instead when I am less well and I am passive, even if always in [a disposition of] love, the others are happy to help and love me. For us it is an experience of humility because we don't reach [this] with our strength. Truly everything serves towards our sanctification. It seems that in this moment Jesus is putting all of us through a school, preparing us for Chiara's visit. (...)"

Despite the distance, she managed to be present in the lives of all those she loved back in Ireland. Eileen Foley, a Gen for many years, got married on 13th July. Lieta lived the day with her. "I remember I went to the hotel from the Church and there was a phone call from Lieta, ringing me to keep Jesus in our midst and to wish me a joyful day," recalls Eileen.

In August she had her last round of chemo. One day by chance she was at the focolare centre when the zone Council was meeting. They knew that she would soon leave for the Delegates' Meeting in Rome and spontaneously asked her to share what her months in Argentina had meant to her. Her communion of soul that day remained for many of them a precious gift. She shared how she had understood that the movement and spirituality was a work of God because everything had gone ahead in Ireland while she was away.

"At this time, God didn't need me in Ireland. He wanted to make me go through a school of life, a school of losing and gaining, because I am certain that if a person knows how to lose well, a gain comes from it. God is love, His will is love.

"These have been months of suffering and intense love and now I feel like a Gen 3, because I got to know the movement when I was fifteen and I always wanted to give everything to God in freedom, not because I had to take vows or follow rules, but freely. And now I feel that God has taken me away from Ireland as if to say to me: 'I am the first in your life. I have to be the first, in full freedom.'"

She told them of her uncertainty for the future. She did not know where she would be, but was not concerned. "So I'm going to Rome without a [final] destination. I feel very detached from Ireland, even if I have it in my heart a lot because for more than thirty years of my spiritual life, practically speaking from when I was 21, I was there and Chiara will go there next year for the first time. But what matters is God, so the deepest experience is that when you get sick and you find yourself before Him (...) you see how much your humanity is mixed with the divine, how much you did for yourself, believing you were doing it out of love for God and rejoicing too. Instead when suffering arrives, love is purer."

Before leaving Argentina, Lieta visited her family, including her brother Eduardo who lived 1200 kilometres away in Nuequen, in the south of Argentina. For a person in her delicate state of health, it was a huge undertaking, but Lieta was determined to see him. "It was a big adventure," Silvina recalls. "They lived far away. We tried to just stay in the present moment, and when the time came, with the strength she had she could do it. It was a continuous exercise not to put limits on her desires or the thoughts that came from her heart."

Lieta also spent a week at Mariapolis Lia with Kuqui and her family, establishing a relationship with her nephews and nieces that would remain forever. There was a going away party too for her in La Plata, with nearly all of her family present. Each of them was thinking that this was probably going to be the last time they saw Lieta but this thought did not mar the joy each person felt, as one by one Lieta sealed the bond with each one.

As the time drew near for her departure she felt particularly upset at the thought of leaving Silvina, who had become like a part of herself, living through the most difficult and traumatic experiences of those months in Argentina. Initially she thought it might be possible for Silvina to come to Rome and hoped to have her great friend at her side, but this was not to prove possible. So with a wrench of the heart, on 14th September 2002, Lieta left Argentina - for the last time.

Chapter 20

Return

On a warm autumn day, Lieta arrived in Rome. To her it seemed a miracle that she had left Argentina and was about to see all her fellow delegates and Chiara once again. She would also see some of her Irish family: Juanita, Stefano (who had taken Bruno's place as delegate) and Paola. Before the meeting she rested for a few days and then took the familiar road to the Mariapolis Centre in Castelgandolfo. She had been here many, many times before, but this time she came with a heightened awareness, living each moment as if it were her last.

Juanita who had lived with Lieta for years in the zone centre in Ireland was anxiously awaiting her arrival. "I waited the whole afternoon in the parking lot outside, so I could see her as soon as she arrived," she recalls. "I remember, I was waiting, waiting. Then at a certain point I heard they had gone to Mass and I went up [to the square at Castelgandolfo] to wait for them. I was waiting outside when they came out. I couldn't believe that it was possible."

Juanita's joy was mirrored all around her. For Lieta it was an overwhelming experience to meet so many people that she loved all at once. That night she found it hard to sleep. She realised that for months her whole life had been concentrated on herself and her health. Suddenly she was confronted with many people, much love. She wrote: "I was hesitant. I didn't know how to act in front of the others who, knowing my state of health, were asking me many questions out of love. Now I have understood that I have to live one hundred per cent and throw myself into this meeting with my whole soul and mind, keeping the balance with my physical strength."

At this point she had been away from Ireland for nearly nine months. Now was the moment to take back her responsibility fully "for as long as it is the will of God". "To have balance, I feel I have to have my heart full and not half full - fully living the will of God each moment," she wrote.

Lieta attended about half the sessions in conference hall B at the Mariapolis Centre in Castelgandolfo. When she tired, she retreated to a little room where she could watch everything through close circuit TV. Her room became an open house.

"She was always loving," recalls Marite, a focolarina from Korea living in London who was present at that meeting. "When she was in bed, she was linked to the hall. Other people discovered this. She welcomed them in. Sometimes there were ten women with her. She had walnuts she had been told to eat to help her memory, but she shared them with everyone, saying 'No, it's for you'."

During the month long Delegates Meeting, Lieta went through various alternative therapies to support her conventional medical treatment. Once a week, Cathy Grue, a focolarina and lifetime friend from Britain, drove her to one of these therapies. Cathy noticed how Lieta had grown in virtue through her illness. "One day something negative had happened and I was inclined to ask 'Why' and have a moan about it, but Lieta said 'Maybe it's better not to talk about it,' and we left it at that."

The gathering settled into a daily routine of updates and planning meetings, interspersed with moments of personal sharing in order to forge those present into one soul - a supernatural family with Jesus in the midst. The delegates became a close family where everything belonged to everyone, and each person lived for the reality and country of the other person.

One day towards the end of the meeting, Lieta decided to share her own experience of her illness and what it had brought about in her soul. She stood and walked to the front of the hall, then sat behind the desk. The eyes of her two hundred fellow delegates looked at her intently. No one moved as a complete stillness descended on the hall. Her voice wavering at the start, and then getting gradually more confident, Lieta thanked them for all their love and prayers which had made it possible for her to be there.

She went on: "It seems to me that through the illness I have been purified. The love of God is more life in me. Before, it was a concept. I chose God-Love in my life, but through this period of suffering the experience has been one of truly believing that God is love. And I have experienced that God's love is not our type of love. It is something else. The love of God is very strong. All of a sudden He wrenched me away from Ireland and I found myself far away. "It was an experience of losing everything. But Mary at the foot of the cross brings her fruits because it seems to me that there have been fruits as never before in Ireland, and in April I heard that Chiara is coming and this is the most beautiful fruit, the greatest gift.

"Then perhaps when you find yourself in front of death in a more real way you see that earlier in your life you did everything because you liked doing it. You did it out of love for God but truly for yourself as well. Instead with this experience you are forced to love God more for God. In the beginning, said Lieta, her love for God through the sickness was very individual, and she experienced the "silence of God".

But after a time she re-discovered the pearl of the Gospel - our brother - and there once more she found the light, the "Paradise of Jesus in the midst".

At a certain point she did not know if she was going towards Paradise, or towards getting better. Then God made her see that she was getting better. She felt tremendous support from Chiara and Gis - who rang and wrote regularly and the other delegates too. She felt she was part of their focolare community too.

"The collective spirituality becomes a reality. Truly we do nothing without our brother," she said. "Every meeting with each brother is sacred. It is that one moment which is not repeated."

As the delegates' meeting drew to a close, Lieta wrote to Chiara. She felt she had been changed by the experience of illness and by the month of "Paradise and refoundation" with the other delegates. Looking ahead to her return to Ireland, she said she counted on Chiara's unity "to go ahead, fixed in the present. I live fully to be a cause of joy for the people I will meet, consuming every suffering with my spouse; losing everything so as to be another Jesus."

Yet as she left, Lieta felt a weight in her heart. She had taken back the responsibility for the movement in Ireland, but did not feel well and was not sure she was up to the task. Drawing Neldi aside, she confided in her. "I feel that I have not borne fruit," she said and began to cry. "A lump came into my throat too," Neldi recalls. "Then she looked at me and said. 'But if I'm not well, I'll return to

Argentina.' You can see that she lived the whole of October not feeling well, the cancer was beginning to come back."

On 21st October, Lieta returned to her beloved Ireland. Her homecoming was a low key affair with just Catherine and Paula waiting for her at Dublin airport. "She didn't want to have a lot of people there. The impact of meeting people took its toll. On the way back a headache had started. It was Halloween and bangers were going off and kids were going from house to house," Paula remembers.

When she reached the Mariapolis Radiosa there was a great celebration. Flowers festooned the big house and the focolare centre. Lieta had said that she would like to rest in the Gen flat of the centre, so with great love the married focolarine had refurbished it. As she arrived Breda, Sarah and Adrienne were just adding the finishing touches. Lieta had been up since 4.00am that morning but she immediately wanted the car to stop so she could give a hug to each one.

Waiting for her in the zone centre were gifts, sweets, wine and cards. Her writing desk had been moved to the ground floor to make her office work easier. Everything looked welcoming and bright. "This house is worthy of Chiara," was Lieta's immediate comment. More gifts awaited her upstairs in her bedroom, including a new sports outfit - complete with track suit pants, a tee shirt and denim jacket - a gift from the other women in the focolare. With her typical spontaneity Lieta immediately wanted to try everything on and then to go and visit the Mariapolis Centre. The others persuaded her to rest. She could see it later.

Fr Tom Norris said Mass at the Mariapolis centre that evening, joined by some more people from the focolare community in Prosperous. There was a special joy. The Mass was a thanksgiving to have Lieta back. "As soon as Mass was over, we thought of going to see the apartment, but immediately Lieta asked Tom to hear her confession. Everything and everyone was important but that was the first thing," remarked Paola.

The others waited and then together they showed her the renovated Gen apartment. She was pleased with all the changes. As the priest blessed the apartment she said, "The priests have given everything because they will give their new house to Chiara so they have the right to stay here when Chiara comes."

Returning from her nine months in Argentina, Lieta had several suit cases with clothes for all seasons. Her first task was to put everything away. "Let's make an inventory," she said to Paola, and they began the task. Then she turned to Paola and said with great humility. "Put a rein on my hurry. Tell me if you think we are doing too much." "I realised that Lieta was indeed changed," Paola recalls.

A few days later she visited a new GP in the nearby village of Clane. At the end of her consultation she surprised the doctor, when she spontaneously turned to her and said "May I give you a hug as we do in my country?"

Each day as the week progressed, Lieta felt less well. Outside it got colder and darker. A pain developed in her back and no matter which way she moved she could not find a position in which she was comfortable. It became a crushing pain. Her way of the cross was beginning.

Chapter 21

Handing on the baton

Lieta's physical pain reached its climax on the night of 30th October 2002. It had been a hard night for everyone. In the sitting room of the focolare, the focolarine and married focolarine had tried to continue their meeting as usual, while each felt inevitably drawn to the room above where they knew Lieta was in great pain. "I can't make it," she had whispered earlier while they frantically tried to find a doctor to come quickly. For three days she had been in pain. For three long nights she had not slept.

The doctor had now been and gone. They had followed his arrival, footsteps up the stairs, muffled conversation with Paula and Lieta in the bedroom above. Sometime later, with relief they heard that she had finally slept, and were about to leave, when there she was, sitting at the top of the stairs. "Lieta" they cried as they rushed up to her. "We thought you were asleep." "I can't sleep. The pain is too strong," she said and began to cry.

"Through all her suffering we had never seen her cry before," recalls Susan. "Surrounding her we tried to do everything, anything to take the pain away. Paula and Lia massaged her back. The rest of us sat in silent tableau around her."

"You don't know how much I love you all," she sighed as she gently tousled Jucemara's curls and touched Adrienne's cheek. "After you used to ring me in Argentina and I heard your voices, I used to cry. Now I feel I am an obstacle. It would be better if I were gone so that everything could go ahead." Tears streaming down their faces, they assured her that this was not so. They reminded her of what Taisaku had said she was to be: "A mountain offering solidity and security to everyone."

"I need to cry," she said. "At times if a spiritual suffering comes you are able to make it pass by loving Jesus forsaken, but with a physical suffering if there is nothing that can be done after many days, it is not easy. ..... When I was in Argentina I always wanted to come back, now I don't know what is happening to me.... In any case I am happy. After the operation I felt so ill, I prayed and I spoke with Jesus. And there you see your soul which is so imperfect. A desire came to me to study theology..."

Then she looked her friends in the eye one by one and said the words that were to remain indelibly printed on their souls: "You have to bring the Work [of Mary] ahead." It was like a testament, a handing over of the baton in the relay race. And looking into her face, so distraught with suffering, each one said a solemn 'Yes' - to Lieta and to God.

Adrienne suggested that she go back to bed, and they would stay with her. Agreeing, she used all her strength to get up and walk the short distance to her bedroom. Another tableau. Lieta sat on the bed. Two of her focolarine behind her, trying to rub away the pain, and four kneeling in front. "We prayed together. We silently assisted in her cry of pain to God. She shared it with us, and we were taken into it with her. Sacred moments. She had shared everything with us for years, now she shared the most precious thing of all - her suffering," recalls Susan.

Almost as if to take her and their minds away from the agony, she said "I never told you my experience of Argentina," and she began to tell them of her new choice of God in suffering over there. One person sang a song of love to Jesus forsaken "Only You remain at the end of the day, only You remain." Lieta relaxed a little. "I think I can sleep now, you can go home," she said.

The next day word came through that there was a room available in a private hospital in Dublin. In great pain Lieta bid a final farewell to the little town of Radiosa in Prosperous.

Chapter 22

Testament

Ten days after her return to Ireland, Lieta was back in hospital again in St Vincent's Private Hospital in Dublin. Looking around her single room and out the window which overlooked a golf course, she said "We are children of the king." She suggested a few things to be bought but then said "Let's not allow ourselves to be taken by consumerism."

She had received a beautiful notebook as a gift and started to write notes about her health so as to be able to update the doctors when they came. That first morning she wrote: "I try to have peace and to be calm. All the others are making unity to me. With them, it is a Paradise with Jesus in the midst with us." That day she had a scan. She was so weak that she has to be brought down on a trolley. For 20 minutes she and Paola waited in the corridor for the test. They both recognised Jesus forsaken in the waiting. "They brought us down too early," said Paola. And Lieta: "Yes."

The scan results were not good and straightaway the doctors began to administer a light dose of morphine to relieve the terrible pain. The next day when Lieta woke up she could not open her right eye. Pressure on a nerve had caused it to close. Nonetheless, her soul was rejoicing. "Let's make a pact to love the whole day. I want to run. I am happy," she told her two companions. Juanita rang and before she even had time to say hello, Lieta told her of her joy and asked her to join in that pact of loving.

"There was a joy in her and among us that was indescribable," Paola recalls. "And yet we continued everything in the greatest normality, having breakfast and then putting the room back in order. Lieta couldn't do much, so she said to me. 'Put this here,' or 'change the position of that other thing,' and with her sense of humour and her capacity to laugh at herself she said, 'Do you see how I'm still capable of bossing you around, even now!'"

That day nine members of the movement were leaving for an important business conference in the west of Ireland on 'Values and Ethics'. One of the delegation, Lorna Gold, was to speak of the Economy of Communion. It was the first time the economic theory born from the spirituality of the Focolare had been spoken of in Ireland at such a prestigious event. Paola Monetta, one of the delegation, rang Lieta in the hospital to tell her about it.

With decision and authority, Lieta told her how to live at the conference. "Go to bring the charism. Do everything in a professional way, yes. Be interested and appreciate everything, but do not be shy. Bring the spirituality of unity and touch those hearts. Do not be silent but shout.... from the rooftops. Be visible. For a long time now we have been quiet and hidden, but now is the moment of visibility."

From her hospital room, Lieta lived for the conference. Afterwards she heard that Lorna's talk impressed the 650 delegates present. It seemed like a coming out to public life of this aspect of the movement.

A few days later she dictated a letter to Chiara, telling her that the test results were not good, but that spiritually she felt under a special grace "free, happy, fulfilled. (.....) In our Ideal there is everything and Jesus forsaken has taken the upper hand in my life".

She told Chiara the latest news: a group of Gen 3 had been to the Irish Parliament and invited the Minister for Children to meet her, the Economy of Communion had been launched at the conference for economists (where they sold 50 books on the topic), a Muslim girl had just returned very happy from a meeting of Muslim friends of the movement. She concluded "Today I feel I have reached the normality of the supernatural, which is Paradise." These were not mere words. Everyone who visited Lieta was impressed to see how she lived the present moment - listening to the person in front of her completely, doing each thing with love.

A pastoral worker from the hospital paid her a visit, and immediately there was a natural and lively relationship with her. She told Lieta and the others about her family and they discussed the situation of the Church in Ireland. "We were like sisters," Paola recalls. Before she left they said a prayer together. "We ask that I can do the will of God and we pray for all those who are in this hospital and who have not accepted their illnesses," Lieta prayed.

Nora, a married focolarina slept over with Lieta one night. In the morning Lieta sat on the edge of bed and one by one she recalled the members of Nora's family, asking about each person. Nora's daughter was fifteen and wanted to go to a disco. Nora did not want to let her go. Lieta listened to her carefully. "Remember what counts is not what you want for your daughter but what God wants for her."

Another visitor told her that her nine year old son had entered a competition and was absolutely convinced he would win the first prize of a playstation. To cushion his probable disappointment, the mother had told her son. "Well, if Jesus wants, you'll win it." Lieta listened in silence, then said "But don't be putting the blame on Jesus." The mother took the point. Never again would she say something like that to her children.

Lieta gave a precious lesson of life to each person: you live as if you were going to die today. Everything done for Jesus. Everything as love for people. Everything in the present. Living this way all the small things, from reading a letter to sipping her juice, became sacred.

That weekend as Juanita and Stefano met hundreds of members of the movement in a school hall in Dublin to update them on the annual Delegates' Meeting in Rome, Lieta rested in her hospital room. The phone rang and Paola picked it up. It was Chiara ringing to see how Lieta was. Lieta, full of joy, took the phone and spoke to her, telling her that she had a lot of hope. "Maybe I will go into remission again..." Hanging up, Lieta immediately thought of telling Juanita and Stefano of her conversation with Chiara. She tried several mobile numbers, but they were all turned off.

In the hall of Manor House school, over two hundred people were listening to Stefano speaking. A telephone went off. Nora rose with embarrassment and made her way quickly to the door. Seconds later she ran back in again, holding the phone, calling to Juanita. "Lieta is on the phone!" Juanita went outside briefly, then came back in and putting the phone on speaker, she held it to the microphone. Lieta told the hall about her chat with Chiara. Everyone was delighted. When the conversation ended there was a burst of spontaneous applause. As she hung up the phone, Lieta turned to Paola. "That's it. This is how the joy of one person is multiplied and becomes everyone's," she said, adding mischievously, "I bet I woke them all up!"

During the evenings of the update weekend a continuous series of extraordinary meetings took place, as one after another, Lieta's 'people' came to see her. They had travelled from the four corners of Ireland for the update and to visit Lieta and were overjoyed to be re-united with her. With a patch over her right eye, she told everyone "I am the first pirate focolarina!"

Sitting on the bed, she brought ahead the work of God in each person - listening intently, offering advice, laughing at jokes. Each one had the impression of a meeting with Jesus in that moment. She was particularly focussed on Chiara's visit in May. She told a Volunteer who lived in the West of Ireland how to prepare the community for the visit. One visitor, a young man, wrote to her afterwards, "For the first time in my life I can honestly say that I understand the present moment. I saw an example of that when I met you, just by being yourself and really living what you believe I can clearly understand the present moment and the importance of it."

The hospital staff was stunned at the number of visitors. When she had arrived they had felt a natural sympathy for Lieta - a woman far from her native Argentina, with no family close by. But they soon realised that here was an extraordinary person. Such was the volume of visitors, that Maureen McNamara, a Volunteer and specialist in bereavement counselling, took up residence as a permanent 'guard' on duty near the lift, to filter visitors, ensure there were not too many at any one time and that they were not disturbing the other patients and visitors.

Among the visitors was Cardinal Cathal Daly. "I was with her in the room the day the Cardinal came to see her and just at that moment someone came to bring Jesus in the Eucharist to her," recalls a Brazilian focolarina, Vaudete. "It was a very strong moment of Paradise, of communion with Jesus and with the Church. Lieta was transformed by happiness, her small face radiant and she said to the Cardinal 'May they all be one'. There I understood that from her little bed, she was continuing to build the Work of Mary as never before."

The Cardinal was moved by the visit too. Afterwards he wrote: "God was truly present, almost palpably present, in her and around her. I was deeply impressed by her serenity and peace: she certainly radiated 'joy and peace in believing'."

For the first two weeks in hospital Lieta concentrated on getting better. "How I want to be here when Chiara comes in May and He can do it," she told a friend on the phone one day, adding, "I only want to do the will of God." Elda, the doctor she lived with in Argentina, arrived and there was talk of a return to Argentina to take up treatment there again. Lieta was unsure. "Let us re-consecrate ourselves to Jesus forsaken," she told Paola Grazia who was her constant companion.

But the next morning when she woke up she felt worse. "The spouse has arrived" she said, then she passed out in her bathroom. She was weak and only able to take sips of liquids like water or fruit juice. She could not sit up in the bed and yet she continued to follow everything - her phone calls, visitors and daily tasks - with all her being.

Later that day, her much loved oncologist rang from Argentina. In silence she listened to him. As she hung up the phone, her expression was thoughtful. "It seemed that I was going to go back to Argentina to recover, but now I have understood - I will stay here and I will prepare myself for the meeting with Jesus and I have a great peace inside."

Paola recalls "In that very sacred moment, I experienced a peace that I never experienced before and I could only thank her for the peace I felt inside that she was transmitting to me too. Immediately Lieta said 'Let's thank Jesus - he is the one who gives peace'. Then she went on in a very normal way, 'Now let's get your bed ready and go to sleep'."

Once a month Chiara held a live conference call with the movement all over the world. It was known as the 'Link up'. The November 2002 Link up was approaching. The day before, Chiara wrote to all the members: "Lieta, the delegate of Ireland has got worse again. It is a great suffering. She is in the most complete peace and she also has hope. But humanly speaking ... I invite you all to ask for a miracle, so that this may happen. Let's ask it all together, each morning at Holy Communion, through the intercession of Foco[20] ." She ended the letter, "So: a miracle for Lieta, if God wants it." Everyone prayed for a miracle. Lieta adhered to this prayer too. The next day from her hospital bed, Lieta listened to the telephone conference call.

"Look Lieta, we are with you!" Chiara told her and the thousands of people listening on the phone. "Today [we've asked] the whole world, through the delegates, to ask for the miracle in the name of Foco, if possible for your full recovery. We wait with faith, with hope. Be at peace. Be happy. I know you already are."

In the spiritual thought that day Chiara shared a strong spiritual intuition she had of the majesty of the Risen Jesus: "He had set aside his infinite greatness out of love for us and he had made himself small, a man among men, like one of us, so small as not to be visible from a plane.

"In rising from the dead, he broke, he surpassed all the laws of nature, of the entire cosmos, and by doing so, he showed that he is greater than all that exists, greater than all that He created, greater than all that can be imagined.... I knew this undoubtedly.... but in this experience it was almost as if I had seen it. My faith became clarity."

Lieta listened. With Chiara she believed in the

power of the risen Jesus but physically she felt so weak. Later that day, nurses came to turn her in the bed. Paula was with them. "You could see she was in the last stages of life. The nurses lifted her and in that moment, the stress was so great that she had the symptoms of a person who was dying. Her head fell back and there was no pulse. It was as if she was gone. Her eyes were open, vacant."

She stayed like that. The nurse said "She's gone." Paula took her head in her arms, spoke and caressed her. She was the only person there, except for the nurse. She thought it was Lieta's last moment. "I said in her ear 'Lieta, will we say a Hail Mary?' I started the Hail Mary and she looked at me. I felt my gaze had to be love. I wasn't panicking. I had to look and accompany her with love. At a certain moment I paused. 'Lieta do you remember the promise we made to Chiara at the Link up today, about the miracle?' Lieta made eye contact with me. I could see the effort in her eyes. It was as if she was defying death. She sucked in a breath with a tremendous effort and within moments her breathing was weak but regular. She had come back. It was as if Chiara had called her back to life. It wasn't the moment for her to go."

Lieta had 'died' for two minutes, but she came back. She had not yet finished her work.

Chapter 23

Dark Night

The next few days were among the most difficult in Lieta's life. Neldi arrived from Argentina, accompanied by Taisaku. Pina who was with Lieta in the Dublin focolare for ten years, arrived from Rome. Gis and Emmaus[21] came to bring Chiara's greetings. Everyone was praying for the miracle of her recovery. Meanwhile her strength diminished by the hour. It was a period of darkness interspersed with light. Lieta was confused. She did not know what to do, where to go - whether to stay in hospital or to return home, whether to live or to die. Her only trust was in Jesus in the midst and in living each present moment.

On a Sunday night she woke up. Nora was with her. In a weak voice she said "Jesus in the midst is worth more than anything. He is too great. He is worth more than our parents, our sisters, brothers, everyone. He is a cathedral."

Then with great calm, she named, one by one, her brothers and sisters. She named a girl who met the movement during its early times in Ireland. She named the husband of a married focolarina. It was the early hours of Monday morning. Nora suggest-

---

[21] Dr Maria Voce (Emmaus) later succeeded Chiara Lubich as President of Focolare when the founder died in 2008.

ed saying the rosary, the Joyful mysteries. "No, we'll say the Glorious ones," Lieta replied. During the rosary she asked the others to pray for all those who were under the 'mantle of Mary' - those who had met the spirituality of the Focolare over the years and gone away, and to ask that they might find their way back.

On Monday morning Adrienne was with her. A nurse was joking with Lieta. "Her face was radiant as I had never seen it before and then she said 'I can't wait.' The nurse asked 'For what?' Lieta didn't answer. Then I said to her: 'What are you waiting for with such expectation?' And Lieta: 'Beauty'. She had opened her eye while she said 'beauty' and she had a smile that I couldn't describe. I said to her 'You are the beauty of which you speak,'" recalls Adrienne.

But later in the day, Lieta's soul was thrown into torment once more. Talking to Chiara on the phone she said: "I don't know what to do in order to leave. I can't manage to die...." She felt she was a burden, that she was stopping everyone from going ahead. Still such was her trust in the presence of Jesus in the midst that by the end of the conversation she was once again at peace. Together they resolved to "love in the present moment". "We live the present moment and Jesus in the midst is that same Jesus who we will see one day. If you see him before me, greet Him for me," said Chiara. "Certainly," replied Lieta.

But that night, the trial returned. This time Paola Grazia was in the room with her. Lieta awoke in the middle of the night. "I feel I'm not love anymore," she told her. Paola reassured her telling her that every gesture, word and action of hers had been love. "Are you sure?" Lieta asked. "Absolutely. I assure you of it," replied Paola. Then with a great trust, Lieta said to her: "Then forward; give me a glass of water, please."

She was still receiving many visitors. Some she had not seen for twenty years and yet when they heard that she was ill, they immediately wanted to re-connect with her. For many she had had a formative influence on their lives. "Her deathbed was like an altar," said Paula Dowd. "It was like her 'office', as if she was at work. She just had to be and listen. I was accompanying people to meet her. There was always a sense of anticipation and then when they were going away, I saw the transformation that happened in them. She had lived in every second of her life, every moment in preparation for the final moment."

She had not forgotten her family and friends in Argentina either, like her good friend Silvina. On Wednesday Silvina was due to call Lieta. Some nights earlier she had dreamt of Lieta, and while they chatted on the phone, Silvina told Lieta about her dream. In it she and Lieta were going along the same road they used to take, Silvina was driving, Lieta navigating.

"I was looking ahead and she was looking at me, without looking at the map. We reached a beautiful park. Everything shone. There were a lot of people waiting in the park and they gave Lieta a big round of applause. Lieta got out of the car and went towards the people. I said 'I'll wait here.' She said 'No, you go ahead and I'll stay.'" Lieta listened intently. "It's beautiful. It is like this, Silvina," she said in a weak voice.

But with darkness on Thursday night, came terror. Lieta sensed a presence of evil and was petrified. She imagined it as a rat. It was a terrifying presence. "Chase him away, send him away," she told Paula who was with her. "Send what away?" Paula asked. "Send him away," repeated Lieta, her breathing agitated. Her eyes were squeezed shut, as if she was having a nightmare. Paula and Elda, her GP from Argentina, told her "Together we are sending him away." "Is he gone?" she whispered. "Yes," said Paula.

"She kept her eyes shut and kept resting. The people in the room were as frightened as Lieta. I felt it was Jesus in the midst who had dispelled whatever needed chasing away," said Paula. Ultimately she slept peacefully. It seemed the final trial was over and Lieta prepared to meet Jesus in person the next day.

Friday: Paula, Elda and Neldi were in the room with Lieta. She had her eyes closed and was not speaking. That morning it had rained very heavily. Suddenly the sun came out and the three of them looked out on the view. It was beautiful. The birds were playing in little water pools and the sun was shining through the trees which sparkled like Christmas trees after the rain.

Neldi, who was holding Lieta's hand, began to describe the beautiful scene. "Lieta, if you could see this. It's like Paradise." And suddenly Lieta said "Let's sing."

A lump came into Neldi's throat as they began to sing the songs of the first times of the movement. "I tried to think of an early Argentinean song, but we were all so moved that we couldn't remember any. It was a moment of true Paradise, a joy, you could touch the presence of Jesus in our midst."

Gis, Juanita and Taisako arrived and Gis took a picture of Taisaku to bring back to Chiara. The focolarine lived that day with a sacred solemnity. They had all got off work to be with Lieta. "One was doing one thing for her, another something else," recalls Neldi. "Then we opened the post which had arrived from different parts of the world, some with photos enclosed. We read them one by one. We put her wardrobe in order."

Lieta spoke very little but her few words had the weight of the divine. At one point Neldi asked her how she was. "Well, through Jesus forsaken," she replied. "I never forgot those words because there was the depth of the Resurrection which is born from love for Jesus forsaken. I told her 'Now I understand why we lived that joy this afternoon.' 'That true joy' said Lieta."

Fr Breandán Leahy remembers his conversation with her that day very well. "Emaciated, she smiled a smile from paradise with all her energy. Then, weakened, our conversation about the trial, how the Evil One has been conquered by the Risen Christ, about how Love conquers all. She repeated three times to me in the final meeting: 'I only have the present moment'."

At 6.00pm many went to Mass. It was the feast of St Cecilia and the readings vividly evoked Lieta and her flight to God. The first reading from Hosea describes a betrothal: "The Lord says this: I am going to lead her out into the wilderness and speak to her heart. There she will respond to me as she did when she was young (......). I will betroth you to myself forever, betroth you with integrity and justice, with tenderness and love." In silence they thought of Lieta upstairs, of Lieta as a seventeen year old with her long flowing hair saying her radical definitive yes to God which never waivered.

The Gospel at Mass was the story of the foolish virgins. "That was Lieta's reading. She always had her lamp burning, for every person," remarked Paula. Juanita commented: "Lieta loved people so much that she would probably have shared her oil with the 'foolish virgins' and stayed locked out with them."

Upstairs in the room, Neldi, Taisaku and Paola were left with Lieta. They were saying the rosary. When they reached the fourth Glorious mystery, the Assumption, Neldi felt urged to tell her sister: "Look Lieta, you are arriving and Jesus and Our Lady are coming to take you. The people from the heavenly Mariapolis[22] will be happy to have you there." Neldi thanked her on behalf of Ireland for what she had done, and then they continued to sing. Soon the others arrived back from Mass. Gis read Chiara's latest link up message about the resurrection and each one lived, could almost touch with their hands, the presence of the Risen One.

Lieta's breathing changed. The end was very near. "We were singing Salve Regina," Paula remembers. "I was doing more nursing things, standing a little behind her, holding her jaw. At a certain moment, I knew her heart had stopped." Around twenty people encircled Lieta's bed, men and women focolarini, Taisaku, priests and other close friends. Every branch of the movement was represented. No one said anything. They accompanied Lieta to the door of Paradise. This time when Lieta left, it was a glorious entry. She had arrived.

---

[22] Heavenly Mariapolis - expression used in Focolare to describe Paradise.

Chapter 24

You have arrived

The morning after Lieta's death, a long fax arrived from Chiara. She said it was her "last letter to Lieta," but the date showed that she wrote it after Lieta's death. She had never written a letter like this before. "Our Lieta," it began.

"Now you are there, you have reached the place where the Sun can never set again. Jesus your spouse has welcomed you into his Paradise...

"Now you are with Jesus whom you longed to reach and see: when you assured me that you were ready for the big 'leap' and you wanted to know from me how best to prepare for this meeting; when, though crushed by suffering, forgetting yourself, you threw yourself in the present moment, into loving all the people who were beside you or who phoned you from far away...

"Paradise was the word which flowered most frequently on your lips."

And then came the great surprise in the letter, an inspiration of the Holy Spirit, that expressed the will of the whole Focolare family in Ireland.

Chiara continued: "Now that you have reached the One you loved the most, and you have received the reward for your labours, remember your sisters and brothers still on the pilgrimage.

"Remember too the splendid zone of Ireland which you helped to build person by person, [together] with its most recent flower: the 'Mariapolis Radiosa' which from now on has to be called 'Mariapolis Lieta'."

The letter was a great joy. That very day Lieta was to be 'waked' in the traditional Irish way at the centre which would now bear her name.

On Saturday afternoon the wake began. Lieta's body was laid out in the main sitting room of the Mariapolis centre, now Mariapolis Lieta and hundreds of people - including whole families, came to say goodbye to her. Sitting around the coffin, there was silence and prayers, music and storytelling: a communal recalling of her life and a communal grieving. There was a very strong atmosphere of the divine. "When I was looking at her in the coffin it seemed that she asked me why I was looking at her dead body when there were so many people to be loved," recalls Máire O'Byrne. "I immediately began to love and instead of feeling the sadness of her death, I felt the joy of her life."

Downstairs people were drinking copious amounts of tea and coffee, shedding tears and laughing as they recalled their own personal favourite story about Lieta. The overriding atmosphere was one of serene joy, even in the midst of sadness. Lieta had reached the One she loved. Small incidents confirmed the veracity of this. Neldi remembered that the previous night, immediately after Lieta's death, she was on her way downstairs in the hospital lift. She was about to ring home to tell the family the news of Lieta's departure. There in the lift, she suddenly felt a special joy and peace. "It was as if Lieta was telling me: 'Be at peace, I have arrived'."

A year later Brian Reynolds stood at her grave in Prosperous and he too experienced the same peace and calm from Lieta. He had known her in Ireland for many years. After he married he moved to Taiwan. On a visit to Ireland, he and his Taiwanese wife had to make a big decision about where they would live. Standing by her grave, Brian asked Lieta for help. "A feeling of complete calm immediately came into my soul," he wrote. "She seemed to be reassuring me that all I had to do was trust in God and that Jesus in the midst would give the right answer. In fact soon it became very clear that the right thing was to return to Taiwan. From that moment on I have kept that sense of peace in my soul, a profound knowledge that I am exactly where God wants me to be, and I thank Lieta for it."

Sunday 24th November 2002 was the day of Lieta's funeral. The church on the crossroads of the small village of Prosperous was packed to capacity.

Hundreds had travelled from all over the country joining local people, who had grown to love Lieta during her time living in the village. On the altar a long line of priests concelebrated the Mass. In the organ loft another large group, young and old, men and women, sang their hearts out. The Mass reverberated with joy and emotion. Lieta's eulogy was read, and after communion three singers performed a new song Padraic Gilligan had written, based around Chiara's words to Lieta: 'This is the Moment'. The congregation listened, stock still.

This is the moment, this is the time.
The journey is over, you've crossed the finish line.
All of the waiting, all of the pain
Vanish forever, along with the rain.

Moment by moment, you knew what to do
Your love for each person was always so new.
Happy by nature, happy by name
You gave yourself to us, again and again.

Now you have arrived
where the sun will shine forever,
The light of your faith, the flame in your heart:
You have arrived.

We don't say goodbye now cos we'll meet again
Pilgrims together in a world without end
In heaven forever with all of our friends
With Mary our mother, we'll live without end.

"When they were singing the song for Lieta after communion, I felt my soul lift with a supernatural joy that Lieta had indeed 'arrived'" recalls Eileen Cregg. "I felt I was spontaneously joyful for her. And then I felt a strong push to say yes, to love as Lieta loved." A woman who travelled from Galway in the west of Ireland spoke of the strong sense of the early Church at the funeral. "It seemed that we too had met together as they had done, to pray and break bread and I also saw and could say 'See how they love one another,'" she wrote afterwards.

Bishop Raymond Field from Dublin, gave the commendation at the end of the Mass and led the procession out of the church to the nearby local graveyard, Killybegs cemetery, which was about a kilometre from the church. Her Irish family wanted to carry the coffin all the way. A rota of very willing men had been organised but when it came to the moment for the coffin to be carried out, the women who had lived with Lieta in the focolare for so long, shouldered its weight and carried her body, under the soft Irish rain, to her final resting place.

Walking in procession behind Lieta's coffin was the whole movement, people of all vocations, a people on the march. It was a deeply moving experience. Clare, a young mother, flew in from France to see Lieta off. "It was a real journey to heaven. I felt we all accompanied Lieta to her new Home in a supernatural atmosphere. It was as if she had taken each one of us by the hand and brought us to the door of

Heaven. It is the first time in my life I really feel I am in Paradise."

Among the crowds of people who gathered in the country cemetery that day was Alve whom Lieta had helped so much when as a seventeen year old she tragically lost her mother. She and her husband had travelled all the way from Cork to be there. Standing by Lieta's grave Alve whispered. "That woman reared me."

"You can speak of a divine love, but first there has to be that human love," she wrote afterwards. "Lieta took me through the most turbulent years of my life because she had courage and grace and truly believed that God loved me even when I couldn't. There were times when I was frightened of her because she wouldn't mince her words in telling me off. She was very straight and said it as it was. But funny enough it is that honesty that now as a mother, I use with my own kids. How blest I have been to have known Lieta Betoño."

Each and every person there that day could repeat Alve's words: "How blest, how blest...." One family, when they heard that the Mariapolis Centre was to be called 'Mariapolis Lieta' immediately decided to move to Prosperous to be part of the little town that bears her name. Máire O'Byrne said Lieta shaped her entire spiritual journey.

"She brought me through some of the hardest,

toughest, situations of my life. She was a master at making herself one. Out of all that, she tapped into the fact that I had always wanted to study theology. She said 'Why don't you go down to Milltown to study?' She wanted a woman and a lay person to study theology. It seemed impossible. I remember registration for the course was finished, but then I bumped into the President and he made an exception for me. It was clearly the will of God. 'Make sure you get a sufficiently high mark so you can do a Masters,' Lieta told me. And I did."

Fr Breandán Leahy said that Lieta was a model for a new form of holiness, a 'collective holiness' based on the unity Jesus prayed for before He died - the unity of "I in you and you in me".

Before she went back to London after the funeral Mari Ponticaccia told an experience of this 'collective holiness'. She was leaving for an update meeting in London, when she heard that Lieta was returning to hospital in Dublin because the pain had returned. She was shocked and upset. On the phone, Lieta consoled her, "Don't worry. You go to your updating and I go to the hospital. It is all the same. I am in you and you are in me."

"To write of Lieta is to recognise the new reality we live, says Fr Breandán - "we in Lieta and she in us. So we can confide in her, entrust people to her, seek her help and pray to her."

Those who knew and loved Lieta have done this since her departure. A year on from Lieta's death, her friend Silvina was working with young children in a nursery in a poor part of Buenos Aires. The father of two of her pupils was always getting drunk and their mother left home. The oldest daughter confided the family's suffering to Silvina. "I told her 'I have a friend in heaven called Lieta and I ask her many things. Let's ask her that your Dad will stop drinking.' A week later the girl came back looking very happy. Her Dad was joining Alcoholics Anonymous..."

Fifteen months after her death, in February 2004, the event that Lieta had ardently longed, lived and maybe even died for occurred, when Chiara Lubich arrived in Ireland. Extraordinary days of illumination and joy followed. In Dublin Chiara addressed over a thousand members of the Irish Focolare family, reminding them that "Jesus is not a perfectionist, but He is love."

She met President Mary McAleese and the then President of the European Union, Taoiseach, Bertie Ahern. There was a conference for business people interested in the Economy of Communion, and in the Irish parliament a cross-party gathering of politicians interested in developing the much overlooked principle of fraternity in politics. In Kildare, under a flurry of snowfall, Chiara gave the February 'Link up' and later that day, in the presence of the bishop of Kildare, Jim Moriarty and the

Italian Ambassador, she officially inaugurated the Mariapolis Lieta.

From heaven Lieta was surely watching this gathering of fruits that she had helped to sow, with a radiant smile. Meanwhile for her spiritual sons and daughters, she remains as a reality among everyone, a Yes to Love in every present moment, with joy - Lieta!

THE END

For information about Focolare, contact:

International

www.focolare.org

Ireland

Focolare Centre,
Curryhills, Prosperous,
Co. Kildare

+353-45-840410

info@focolare.ie

Great Britain

Focolare Centre for Unity,
69, Parkway, AL8 6JG
Welwyn Garden City

+44-208-6718355
wzclondon@btconnect.com

30, Langside Drive,
G43 2QQ Glasgow

+44-141-6373316
focolareglasgow@talktalk.net

USA

Mariapoli "Luminosa",
200 Cardinal Road , Hyde Park,
NY 12538

+1-845-229-0230 ext.133 (eve. ext.187)
czf.luminosa.NY@focolare.us

Argentina

Mariápolis Lía - O'Higgins
(Buenos Aires, Argentina)

+54 236-4448505
mariapolis@mariapolis.org.ar

Susan Gately is a journalist specialising in social, family and religious affairs. A former lawyer, she spent five years as editor of the online news service of *catholicireland.net*. She writes for the *Irish Independent, Irish Catholic, the Universe, Reality* and *Living City*, and does multi-media reports for *Catholic News Service* in Washington. She is author of *God's Surprise - The New Movements in the Church* (Veritas 2012) and a long time member of Focolare.

Susan is married to Aidan with two children, and lives in Kildare, Ireland.

Acknowledgements

I would like to acknowledge with gratitude all the people who helped bring *Like the Sunshine* to fruition - Lieta's family, particular Neldi Betoño, who spent hours telling me stories of her younger sister; all those who gave me letters she had written them or so willingly shared stories of the way Lieta touched their lives.

I thank my beloved husband Aidan Gately and Juanita Majury for their guidance and encouragement throughout and the constructive critiques they provided of an earlier version of the book. I thank Brendan Purcell, Máire O'Byrne, David Hickey and Marian Gilligan who guided the later version, and Breandán Leahy for his great editing work.

I owe a huge debt of gratitude to Alan Gabriel, who designed the book and provided so much assistance guiding us through the hoops of publishing.

Thanks to Padraic Gilligan for his advice on presentation and marketing, and Tony Curtis for the great cover.

Finally a huge thank you to my family - Aidan and sons, Donnacha and Michael, for the tremendous support they give me in all I do.